Leading edge thinkers
*The Evolutionary Gl*

"Any time you choose to delve into brain functions, you are in for some deep study and thought. It is no different with Albert Garoli's *The Evolutionary Glitch* because he takes us deep within neurobiology and quantum physics. Combine that with ancient wisdom and modern psychology and you get a thorough understanding that our emotional, mental and physical health is driven by social conditioning and learned experiences.

"There is so much more to this book! Garoli provides a developmental program and understanding that is time-sensitive, cutting-edge, and a forerunner in the field of neuropsychology. Our society is finally grasping the fact that our behaviors, actions, and thoughts are driven by our internal conflicts. Albert Garoli, in *The Evolutionary Glitch* gives us the insight needed so we can make the changes within ourselves and create our own world that is problem-free."

Irene Watson, *Reader Views*

"Through fifteen years of proof-thirsty work, Albert Garoli, author of *The Evolutionary Glitch*, brings into focus an ancient 'glitch' in the common psyche, named the persona.

"Assembled out of our cultural experiences and acting like a virus, this persona infects our emotional, mental and physical health. It isolates us from our natural way and from each other, sabotaging fulfillment.

"Fusing modern neurobiology, quantum physics and ancient wisdom, the author provides exercises to break down these ingrained destructive neural pathways, so that we may once again be connected to our essential nature.

"With direct application to Psychology, Vitality, Sustainability and Community, this manual for self-discovery provides a sound platform for self-challenge and a daring opportunity for us rise above the root of our problems."

*Rowan Gorringe, Nutritionist & Herbalist*

"Once in a while, a book comes along that changes everything. *The Evolutionary Glitch* was that book for me. This book gave me a whole new way of looking at the world, myself, and the people around me. Reading its pages was like removing the blinders from my eyes for the first time, that I didn't even realize were there.

"Written in a user-friendly, easy-to-understand way, this book has become my user manual for life. Since reading *The Evolutionary Glitch*, I see the world by its terms. I am armed with the knowledge about Personas; this helps me when I interact with people because I recognize the Persona in them, as well as the Persona in myself. I have become acutely aware of the signs in my life, and am getting better all the time at following them.

"*The Evolutionary Glitch* doesn't only provide life-changing information, it actually gives step-by-step exercises and tools to use to change destructive habits, and get back on track with your true life goals. *The Evolutionary Glitch* is a book that I come back to time and time again, and I always get something new and useful out of it. Albert Garoli has given the world a great gift with this book, and how different the world would be if everyone could read it!"

Christelle Jenkin

"Albert Garoli brings a new concept his insightful look into man's love affair with his Ego. Garoli's 'persona' looms over each chapter bringing pitfalls and a hypothesis of *The Evolutionary Glitch* which remains the donning of humanity's proverbial 'rose-colored glasses' and the failure to realize he can choose to remove them at any moment. Garoli's process of 'clearing the conscious awareness of its superimpositions' works well to acknowledge and confront man's 'evolutionary malfunction.'"

Barbara Sinor, Ph.D.,
author of *Gifts From the Child Within*

# THE
# EVOLUTIONARY
# GLITCH

## RISE ABOVE THE ROOT
## OF YOUR PROBLEMS

Dr. Albert Garoli

For information or for international orders, please visit:
www.TheEvolutionaryGlitch.com

Production, composition, and copyediting by Daniella Remy
Editing and proofreading by Kaia Roman
Cover photograph and design by Marilena Chiappalone
Photography by Allen Cooper, www.allencooperphotography.com


Library of Congress Cataloging-in-Publication Data

Garoli, Albert, 1972-
The evolutionary glitch : rise above the root of your problems / Albert Garoli.
p. cm.
Includes bibliographical references and index.
ISBN-13: 978-1-61599-017-7 (trade paper : alk. paper)
ISBN-10: 1-61599-017-8 (trade paper : alk. paper)
ISBN-13: 978-1-61599-018-4 (hbk. : alk. paper)
ISBN-10: 1-61599-018-6 (hbk. : alk. paper)
1. Personality development. 2. Self-management (Psychology) I. Title.
BF723.P4G37 2010
155.2'5--dc22                              2009049536

Published by
Loving Healing Press, Inc.
5145 Pontiac Trail
Ann Arbor, MI 48105
USA

Loving Healing Press

Tollfree 888-761-6268          www.LHPress.com
Fax 734-663-6861              info@LHPress.com

Distributed by: Ingram Book Group, New Leaf Distributing, Bertram Books (UK), and The Hachette Group (EU)

# *Acknowledgements*

I believe it thanks to the people in my environment that I have the ability to grow, succeed, and move on to new endeavours. It is because of their constant love and support that I have the motivation and energy to achieve and venture ever forward.

Of all the help received, Daniella Remy, the chief editor of this work, is surely the empirical embodiment. I would like to thank her deeply for her capacity to clearly understand my thoughts and models and to make them understandable for others.

This book also wouldn't have been possible without the dedicated and diligent help of Kaia Roman, whose support and detail orientation helped transform the ideas into a reality. Her insight, awareness, and meticulousness provided the fine tuning needed to make this book the success it is.

In addition, I am indebted to the community of people in Stezzano, Italy, and Byron Bay, Australia, who provided supportive ideas, reviews, and encouragement throughout this project.

I would like to also extend my thanks to Allen Cooper for his creativity and photographic talent that provided the artistic touch this book needed, as well as Carina Remy for her illustrations despite the little time available in her very busy schedule.

# *Preface*

The natural tendency of every living being is to survive and strive toward a direction: this is the path of life. An evolutionary path is imprinted in our genes and it is up to us to discover it and make the most of it. Our genetic disposition and its natural tendencies express our purpose in life; our life goal is marked in our cells.

Through a long and extensive study of the electrical properties of bodies, tissues, and reflexes, particularly following the footprints of modern pioneers of electro-physiology such as Professor Harrold Saxon Burr, Reinhold Voll, and Biophysicists like Alexander G. Gurwitsch and Fritz-Albert Popp, I have formulated a pragmatic theory on an evolutionary malfunction in our thinking processes. This hindrance to the natural process of adaptation and development acts like a "glitch" in human "evolution."

Ancient Chinese philosophy expressed the concept of evolution through the idea of "the way," a particular subjective predisposition to evolve. Whereas modern thought considers the goal of life to be the acquisition of materialistic goods, the way to evolve in natural environments is to be in harmony with the surroundings, to function in synchronicity with the greater whole. Just like the cells of a body have individual functions that work in synchronicity with all the other cells for a healthy body to work properly, each person's individual goals should work in harmony with group goals. Understanding the reciprocal interaction between individual and group functions sheds light on a second concept. Not only should we avoid individualistic objectives and discover what we can do to contribute to the betterment of the group over the long-term, but we should also see that our unique goals of life seem to be imprinted in our cells as functional for the greater whole.

As a practitioner and teacher of Traditional Chinese and Oriental Medicines, I found many similarities between ancient epistemological explanations of natural laws of evolution and modern biology, psychology, and physics. However, a major discrepancy was found between modern thought and traditional medicines in regards to perceptions of the evolution of the central nervous system humans use to build their map of reality. With the help of new findings, this book provides an analysis of the source of our future orientation and destiny. This concept was known as "Ming" in Traditional Chinese Medicine, and refers to ancient traditional paradigms of vitality thought to be the director of life at the cellular level.

This book provides a clear and detailed description of our evolutionary flaws, engaging in the explanation of how our destiny and future orientation is largely influenced by our behavior in response to our environment. It also provides some prototypical techniques we can use to get rid of these flaws so we can finally resonate with our life goals.

For the past decade, I have conducted extensive research in biological learning models. With the data collected from thousands of patients, combined with my studies on expert systems and artificial intelligence systems, I have learned how cells adapt to their environment. Most interestingly, I have come across two main problems: the discovery of how much the environment can program us, and how wrong conditioning can alter the way we learn.

*I came to understand that good, healthy people are those who have learned properly from life, whereas others have made mistakes in their method of learning. It became evident that there is an "evolutionary glitch" in our neural network that is at the root of human physical and mental suffering.*

By explaining how to uncover the "glitch" in our central nervous system, this book shows how to express natural inborn tendencies and the positive effects that a rebuilt conscious mind has to offer. In the view that an "evolutionary glitch" is at the base of human physical and mental suffering, this book provides some revolutionary concepts and life changing models that anyone can harness through practice. Most importantly, drawing on the study of Phenotypology (the science that studies the effect of the environment on an organism), this book uncovers the root of all your troubles: your conditioned neural network.

In this book, I have merged major fields of human research such as physiology, neurobiology, cognitivism, general systems theory, and traditional medicines and philosophies, while keeping the terminology and explanations as simple as possible. In order to avoid distraction from the progressive and subjective processes introduced in the book, not all of the scientific research has been included. However, the scientific background for the concepts presented in this book are available at **www.holonomics.info**

Some of the suggestions in this book may seem challenging. Unlike typical self-help approaches, I chose not to theorize but rather to focus on applicability in a concise and straightforward manner. Likewise, rather than discussing this approach on a theoretical level, I highly encourage all readers to experiment and try the exercises, challenge themselves, and leave dialogue, opinions, advice, and proposals until the concepts have been understood.

The principles and practices provided in this book are simple and direct and often obvious; so obvious that we have lost the habit of paying attention to them. One of these principles is that the actual state of people's health, welfare, and success is the result of their past actions. This seems to be such a simple concept but it is so simple that it becomes rarely applied in our approach to physical and psychophysical well-being. For instance, in our overmedicated society, rather than looking at what brought us our conditions and stopping those bad behaviors and attitudes, we silence the symptoms with chemicals. We study everything about pathology and very little about healthology.

This book is written with the vision of a new future, where people are taught to know themselves rather than being conditioned to distract their focus from what really matters. The motto of traditional oriental philosophies truly captures the essence of this book:

*It is more important to identify which type of person grows a disease, rather than finding which type of disease grows in a person. In order to heal, you must not cure the symptoms but the temperament.*

It is for this exact reason that when we dig deeply enough into human disease, suffering, and misery, we discover a leading pattern; a pattern that has specific roots in our attitude towards life. There is an "evolutionary glitch" in our thinking process that has separated modern humans from nature. Nature has provided simple rules of communication that are there for us to understand as long as we are humble enough to comprehend and follow them. When we listen closely to what nature has to say, we can be guided in the right directions, follow the way to a better and brighter future, and live harmoniously.

# Contents

**Introduction**                                              1

**Chapter 1 — Know Thy Stance**                               7

    Your Bow and Arrows                    10

    6 Causes of Misfire                    10

    It All Stems from Your Attitude        12

    Assessing Your Stance                  13

**Chapter 2 — Know Thy Foe**                                  15

    How We Become What We Are Not          18

    Why We Remain What We Are Not          24

    Viral Minds                            29

    Starting on the Right Foot             30

**Chapter 3 — The Glitch**                                    33

    The Mask                               36

    The Fall of Man                        41

    The Contaminated Mind                  41

    The Brain Trap                         43

    The Formation of the Mask              44

    *The Ephemeral: Sanguine Persona*      51

    *The Grinding: Lymphatic Persona*      57

    *The Controlling: Nervous Persona*     65

    *The Egocentric: Melancholic Persona*  73

    *The Rebellious: Bilious Persona*      81

    *The Minimalist: Phlegmatic Persona*   89

    Reminder: The Persona is Not You!      97

**Chapter 4 — When Coping Becomes Evading**          99

    Coping Strategies          102

    The Solution          107

**Chapter 5 — Removing the Mask**          115

    Nigredo          119

    Albedo          126

    Rubedo          130

**Chapter 6 — Your Inner Compass**          135

    5 Internal Attitudes (W.I.S.E.R.)          140

    5 External Attitudes (R.E.A.D.Y.)          142

    Skeptic Poison          153

    Become W.I.S.E.R. and R.E.A.D.Y.          154

**Chapter 7 — Your Resonant Way**          157

    Identification and Resonance          159

    Resonant Wave Patterns          163

    Determining Your Goal          166

    Assessing the Quality of Your Goals          167

**Chapter 8 — Encompassing Everything Under the Sun**          171

    What is Killing the Hero System?          174

    Continuation is Motivation          176

    Mind-Opening Exercises          177

    A Broader Mind, A Broader Heart          178

    Life Goal Scale          181

    Meet the Challenge          184

    The All-Encompassing Way          187

    Becoming a Hero          189

**Conclusion**          193

# Introduction

Why do some people strive for improvement and succeed, while others continue to live their lives in a condition they are unhappy about?

Why are some people generally healthy with a good capacity to recover from any stress or illness, while others maintain an unwanted state of frailty or disease?

What is the element that makes some people excel in their accomplishments and others fail in what they want from life?

Why do we build more schools, more philosophical systems, and more sources of information, yet continue to have the same problems our ancestors had thousands of years ago?

When we evaluate ourselves, look at our bodies in the mirror, or at the people around us, we can't help but notice that the entire human population differs in shape, size, physical quality, talent, and achievement. We sometimes perceive that people who excel in their activities use some form of natural talent, knowing how to make the most of their personal qualities; we admire them yet we do not necessarily do the same. It seems that successful, healthy, and motivated people find the best way to express their core beliefs and intrinsic worth, maximizing what they can become. They seem to have a driving force, as well as a strong sense of integration or belonging; they seem to do what they were born to do.

It is human nature to seek improvement, whether for personal health, politics and social order, music and art, technology and engineering, or our own personal abilities to push ourselves to the limit. Humans have always attempted to excel in their abilities to go higher, farther, faster, more precisely, more efficiently, and so on. But only some people experience and express the drive for accomplishment to enhance the current state of personal and collective life with attempts to achieve excellence in their triumphs, amplitude in their knowledge, and brilliance in their actions. What drives them?

The Chinese have a word to describe the ideal state of a human being: the "Ren Jen," or the "real human." Chinese philosophy has carried through the millennia the concept that human beings evolve towards their real nature: the nature of becoming "human." To them, an individual endowed with real "humanity" is characterized by empathy, social integration, and correct psychophysical balance. In this view, priority is placed on personal expansion and synergetic work with others, rather than a desire to climb the social ladder or detach one's self from one's fellows. This is the principle of empathy, which permeates through all Buddhist philosophies under the name of "compassion." Mankind was meant to evolve into a more "human" race. Something went wrong along the evolutionary process and it is the principal aim of this book to investigate this "glitch."

This book examines a new perspective on the very nature of our natural performance, which goes beyond popular self-improvement regiments of diet, exercise, or self-help thoughts. Many books you can find under the class of "self-help" can actually become self-entanglement because they provide unrealistic expectations and predetermined ideas of what we should desire, which are often not adaptable to everyone. There are certain psychological mechanisms that keep humans in darkness, depression, and solitude, no matter how rich and wealthy we can become.

Any effort undertaken without the consideration of our real physical and cognitive limits and opposed forces is often a pallid mirage. The idea that we can do whatever we put our minds to sells well because it makes people feel momentarily good and dream about omnipotence. Unfortunately, it often leaves people with the bitterness of delusion, denying their current state of affairs. Instead, our perceived limits should be an indication of how we should concentrate our efforts, where external forces point to our bearings. As organisms, we live in very precise and definite parameters such as the ratio of gas we inhale, our blood pH, and our body temperature. Not everything can simply be whatever we wish.

## *Real Self-Help Starts With Self-Challenge*

Real self-help comes from the identification of our own innate tendencies, our parameters through the previous recognition of our natural limitations, the strategies to overcome them, the needs of the people around us, and the identifications of our adversaries. This is the general guideline proposed for positive evolution. This is why this book should not be considered self-help, but rather self-challenge.

The first chapter begins with a straightforward and simple definition of your actual condition in order to demonstrate how attitude plays a vital role in your orientation towards life. Our past behaviors bring us our current position in life, or stance. They have made us what we have become. Assessing the past will shed light on the causes of previous unsuccessful enterprises, and give insight into how to aim for the future.

Chapter 2 will expose the flaws of modern thinking revealing that our current path of "evolution" is not actually the best scenario for human beings. Our flaws have often led us to be discontent with what we have, incapable of expressing our given potential, and confused or obscured by a bombardment of external influences. We have been conditioned to adhere to unrealistic standards of beliefs, behaviors, and abilities. We have been taught to want what we don't need and to be something we're not. We have been conditioned to neglect our natural indicator of what is "good" or "bad." We have been taught to copy given models rather than observe our natural tendencies, recognize ourselves, and learn what we were born to do. This chapter will identify the major sources of interference hindering our evolution.

The third chapter is dedicated to revealing the root of your problems: the self-molded mask of the Persona. Your body is the vessel of your innate goals and tendencies, the molecular expression of your natural desires and attitudes, but is sabotaged by an acquired neuronal entity that hinders its progress. This chapter will delve into the core of human problems and will compare human Personae to acquired virus-like mental tendencies. It will show how the Persona is the exact cause of personal derangement from goals and achievements, as well as the source of social disintegration.

The fourth chapter analyzes the various coping strategies are formed to overcome challenges and how these strategies are used by the Persona. Understanding how you naturally react to stress will help you understand the strategies you adopt to survive the tests of life. Adversities overcome by one generation are solved with similar tactics by the progeny who have acquired the methods and attitudes by imitation. Learning why you react in different ways to the challenges of life not only helps your positive progress but also assists the correct development of your offspring.

Chapter 5 will identify the methods best used to rid yourself of the power the Persona has over you and embrace your true nature. Like a remedy for an illness, this chapter will provide exercises you can do to progress toward a better functioning self. Understanding your innate reaction to the environment and your natural tendencies will teach you how to read your "path" and change direction when you need to.

Inspired by past philosophies, Chapter 6 will provide a general outline of what you can do to remedy your social conditioning with emphasis on internal strength and congruence. This chapter will provide the core virtues you'll need before focusing more specifically on your body, your mind, your goals, your values, and your overall potential. The old but reliable attitudes described in this chapter will give you a new point of view on how to harness your human side so that, by the end of the book, you will have definite guidelines to refer to. This chapter also provides a quick checklist of actions to perform in order to detect your natural indicators.

With the help of the seventh chapter, you will understand how your cells resonate with your environment. By understanding the human organism as a homogeneous and harmonious whole in which your body and natural orientation work together to create the individual that you are, you will come to understand that your real goal is easy to detect because it is literally "written" in your cells. This understanding will help you to follow your feelings as indicators, to identify the "resonant situation" that best suits and motivates you. You can recognize and hone in on these resonances to walk the path of your predispositions. Nature granted us a tool to determine our future orientation and it is up to us to use it.

The eighth chapter delves into the structure of life goals that drive people to be great human beings. The motivation behind extraordinary achievements is explained in the context of the survival of the species. Using the approach of harnessing tension and stress as sources of motivation, rather than a mechanism to hinder advancement, this chapter will help you understand how to propel yourself forward with direction and drive to achieve goals that are larger than yourself.

By the end of this book, you will have learned that you are born with a unique direction in life that has a tendency to unfold, even if you don't know it. You will notice that moving forward in the right direction and pursuing your unique path requires you to be attentive and adhere to the signs that your life and your body present to you. The sum of the signs constitutes your destiny. It is your challenge in life to discover it, pursue it, and master it.

# Chapter 1
# Know Thy Stance

*"Success is to be measured
not so much by the position
that one has reached in life
as by the obstacles which he
has overcome."*

Your stance is where we begin. Just like when you read a map, you need to start with your current location before you know where to go and how to get there. Your stance is made of your geographical location, your home and community, your family relationships, your friendships, your job, your activities, the goals you had in the past, the goals you have for the future, and everything else about your present situation. This is the point where you are at, in this very instant. Take a moment to think about your current stance. Is there a reason why you have chosen to stay in that position?

The way you reacted to the happenings in your life has modified your genetic makeup into what you are now. This is called your *Phenotype*, the result of your genetically inherited body plus the way <u>you</u> reacted to the environment. The moment you find yourself in is a clear reflection of your past and current attitudes. The attitude you have had so far in life brought you to where you are now, giving you the possessions you have, modifying your body to the shape it has now, establishing the activities you are performing now, and it is pushing you toward a specific direction.

Whether you realize it or not, the attitude you have represents the kind of experiences you expect. If your attitude is negative, you will expect negative incidents. If your attitude is positive, you will expect constructive and positive events. While your attitude is the approach you had in life so far, your mindset is what you used to respond to events. Your actions then obtained what you originally anticipated. The result of your attitude is therefore your *Stance*. Your stance is your actual position in time and space, the result of all previous purposes you had set in motion in your past.

## *Your Bow and Arrows*

To understand the dynamic of how we achieve goals based on our attitude and stance, imagine you are an archer. You possess a bow and a set of arrows and will follow this sequence in order to use your tools:

1. The arrow is loaded.

2. The bow is held and put into tension.

3. The arrow is directed and aimed at a target.

4. The decision of letting go is carefully operated.

Once the arrow is on its way to the target, the result of your actions will take place, even if you suddenly realize that the way of the arrow is not what you wanted it to be. You can't stop an arrow in mid-flight.

In this analogy, your bow is your motivation. The arrows are the actions you need to perform. The direction is your life course, and the target is the goal you want to reach. Your attitude is your confidence to hit your target, and your stance is your position in life. Now take the time to analyze your situation: do you like it completely?

If you do, there is no need to read this book. If you don't, carry on and investigate what could have procured a situation that you are not completely happy with or that you might want to change. If what you have right now is not what you want, then your attitude that brought you here had inherent flaws and your actions were misfired.

## *6 Causes of Misfire*

1. If your direction was good and you had proper arrows but your bow was not in tension, you did not reach your target. You were missing your motivation.

2. If your direction was good and your tension strong but you had no arrows, there was nothing that could hit the target. Words alone don't achieve; you must act.

3. If your bow was in tension and you had arrows but your aim was off, you missed your target. The result may have become different from what you expected.

4. If your bow was in tension, your aim correct, and your arrows were loaded but you did not let go, nothing could have reached your target. Letting go of the tension at the right moment allows propelling force.

5. If your tension was excessive you might have broken your bow and impeded the process. You should have maintained a more balanced tension.

6. If you aimed correctly, with a tensed bow, and you let go but the arrows were faulty, the course of action failed to reach your target. You should have obtained the proper tools for proper performance.

This analogy is a simple structure but it requires a lengthy introduction to guide you to the real result. Therefore, bear the

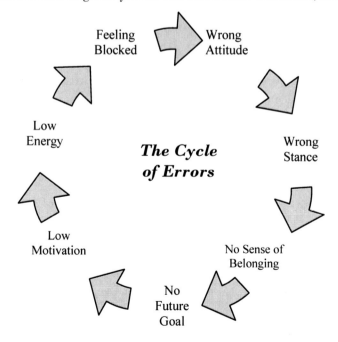

Feeling Blocked

Wrong Attitude

Low Energy

**The Cycle of Errors**

Wrong Stance

Low Motivation

No Sense of Belonging

No Future Goal

bow and arrow example in mind throughout your reading, because your "bow" is the source of your will power.

If you have ever felt stuck in life, with a great sense of fatigue, a severe illness, or a strong lack of motivation, you have experienced a wrong stance. But have you ever thought about how you got there?

Feeling blocked and exhausted has its origin in low metabolic and endocrine energy outputs. This is accompanied with less dopamine release, less adrenaline, less serotonin...less life. Low energy has a root in a low motivation, caused by a bleak or absent orientation. When we do not aspire for anything, we simply do not see how our actions might make a difference in our life, in society, or in our external conditions. This is caused by the feeling that you don't belong in your social environment, no longer having the motivation to perform at your best.

## It All Stems from Your Attitude

*"Our greatest glory is not in never falling but in rising every time we fall."*
*— Confucius*

When you feel blocked and frustrated in your life, it's most likely because you have no energy to move forward and you feel that the resources you have are lower than the ones required to achieve a goal. However, because of the strong influence an environment can have, when you identify with the environment you become like your environment, both natural and social. When you feel like your environment is an important part of you, you naturally develop a desire to take part in its development. When something happens to your environment or to your loved ones, it is natural for you to develop a desire to help and protect the things for which you are personally involved in and committed to. Your motivation to contribute to the wellbeing of your surroundings lies in your close identification with it. If you have no sense of ownership and belonging for your environment, you will not want to change it. It all boils down to having a wrong stance and, more specifically, an incorrect attitude. In the end, the vicious cycle continues unless you decide to break the pattern.

Life is enhanced when a clear, solid, and positive future

orientation is detected. However, it is vital to realize that many interfering influences exist around you to purposefully sway your stance and hinder your future orientation. Most modern societies, through their overly controlling attitudes and corrupted chains of command, make citizens feel frustrated, depressed, and hopeless. As such, citizens are even more controllable and manipulated as a working force and group of consumers. It is extremely interesting to consider how often the same social structures that fight crime and social disorder are the ones that really initiate it.

Your stance is affected by the decisions you made under the influence of external persuasion and social manipulation and the next chapter will therefore shed light on the origin of this heavy interference.

---

### Assessing Your Stance

To find your future orientation, begin by locating and evaluating your stance. Take a sheet of paper and begin answering the following questions honestly. Feel free to add what you deem necessary to sincerely evaluate your stance.

- Do you feel integrated in the community you live in now?

- Do you like the people around you? (family members, friends, colleagues, neighbors, etc.)

- Do you feel satisfied with the outcomes of your efforts?

- Do you have clear goals to strive for?

- Do you like the natural environment of where you live? (climate, nature, etc.)

- Do you feel responsible for the conditions of your environment?

- Do you like your role in society?

- Do you agree with the activities of your government?

"What is needed is a relativistic theory, to give up altogether the notion that the world is constituted of basic objects or building blocks. Rather one has to view the world in terms of universal flux of events and processes."

— David Bohm

# Chapter 2
# Know Thy Foe

*"Society is one vast conspiracy for carving one into the kind of statue it likes, and then placing it in the most convenient niche it has."*

Take the time to reflect on the following questions and answer them truthfully. You don't need to worry about what anyone else is thinking so you should be as honest as possible. Catch yourself lying and maybe you should wonder why.

♦ Are you doing what you feel you want to do or what you think you should do?

♦ What is your true personal goal in life?

♦ Is what you're doing with your life *really* beneficial to you?

♦ Is what you're doing with your life *really* contributing to a greater good?

♦ How much of what you're doing is for the recognition, for the money, or for the prestige?

♦ How much of what you do is to be true to yourself?

You may have found it easy to reply quickly to these questions but not easy to answer them with full integrity. Integrity is the congruence of internally consistent codes of moral attitudes, beliefs, and principles. People believe in social rules, religious principles, ethical codes, legal ideologies, and behavioral guidelines but often forget how it is that we came to learn and accept them. We often find ourselves following socialized ideals.

Though we may know about culture as the elusive structure that directs patterns of human activity, we often overlook or disregard its origins and purpose. We therefore become upholders of *erroneous truths*, dictated by traditions and the business of civilization, and thus disregard our internal congruence. Cultures and subcultures have a tendency to impose "models" and beliefs about "perfection" or "the right way." Desirability and perfection has been constructed by cultural philosophy or the market/media and is intended to get the population to behave in a definite standard way. For those who are willing to go against the status quo, a solution is available.

*The biggest barrier lies in our culture,*
*but the strongest barrier lies in our*
*acceptance of culture.*

The British psychologist Oliver James relates the stimulation of artificial needs to the rise in what he coins *affluenza*[1]. The manipulative methods of the advertising industry encourage a conviction of unattainable standards of achievement measured by our financial success, material possessions, and social hierarchy, which lead to more prominent levels of inequality. The feeling of being unable to reach the top of the totem pole results in alienation, distress, depression, and sometimes psychological disorders with the possible outcomes of self-medication through drugs, alcohol, TV watching, shopping, or antisocial behavior. If this is you, you have been successfully brainwashed by the dominant social agenda, by your foe.

## How We Become What We Are Not

To understand how we get influenced, we first have to comprehend the natural learning processes. Going beyond our natural instincts with which we were born (instinct to eat, to seek shelter, to obtain affection, to avoid death, etc.), we also use our cognitive processes to acquire new knowledge and skills as tools for survival. Throughout the ages, social conditioning has generated what Professor Philip Zimbardo calls the *Lucifer Effect*[2], the frightening effect of how good people can turn evil. Religions and political propaganda, education, destructured modern societies, and strict impositions of institutionary systems have played and continue to play major roles in conditioning us to the point of becoming what we are not. Social rules are like maps, but even the most skilled navigator is exposed to grave danger when he uses the wrong map.

### Conditioned Behavior

Ivan Pavlov, a Nobel Prize winner in 1904 for his experiments on digestion, was fascinated by the study of involuntary reflexes that continuously brought him distinctions in the fields of medicine and physiology. One of his most famous experiments with dogs exposed the notion that we can purposefully "program" a response to a selected stimulus. It began with his

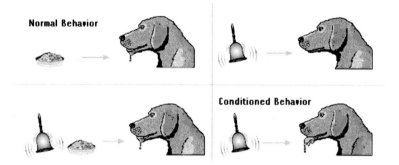

Normal Behavior

Conditioned Behavior

observation that the dogs were salivating without the proper stimulus of food. He later remarked that the dogs were in fact reacting to the sight of the lab coats that they associated to the eminent arrival of food. He tested his theory by attempting to get the dogs to react to the sound of a bell rather than the lab coat. He would ring a bell every time the dogs were fed. As long as the bell rang within a certain time frame to their meal, the dogs became trained to associate the sound of the bell with food. Eventually, the mere sound of a bell ringing triggered a drooling response.

The association of a stimulus to an expected response is what Pavlov coined Classical Conditioning. The reverse effect can also occur when the conditioned stimulus (the bell) is presented too often without the proper unconditioned stimulus (the food) ultimately leading to an absence of drooling and a new learned behavior that the bell no longer means food is about to arrive[3].

We can see extensions of this today, especially with advertising and marketing techniques. Major food chains, for instance, have used specific colors, logos, music, and other triggers to condition the population to emit a desire to purchase their product. The ultimate goal is to use cues that address any of the five senses to trigger associated memories in consumers. Often, when one cue is triggered, others follow (like a logo that reminds you of the commercial, that gets you singing the marketed tune, that makes you think about the product being sold). For instance, what do the following trigger in you?

♦ The sound of a bag of potato chips being ripped open

♦ The color *Ferrari Red*

- The music of *Jingle Bells*
- The smell of coffee

## Programmed Thoughts

Unlike classical conditioning which triggers instinctive behaviors to a selected stimulus, operant conditioning is a technique that uses expected consequences to direct actions. In the mid 1900s, B.F. Skinner conducted experiments in which a lab rat was placed into a box (later termed the Skinner Box) in which the action of pressing a lever would result in the release of a food pellet[4]. It did not take long for the rat to learn that if it pressed the lever it would receive food, so the experiments were extended to the lever working only when a certain light shone, wrong levers leading to mild electrical shocks, or a series of levers having to be pressed sequentially. The result of his extensive experimentation led Skinner to understand that behaviors can be conditioned with specific reinforcers to increase behavior and punishments to decrease behavior:

- *Positive Reinforcement:* Something "good" is "given"
- *Negative Reinforcement:* Something "bad" is "taken away"
- *Positive Punishment:* Something "bad" is "given"
- *Negative Punishment:* Something "good" is "taken away"

We commonly see this kind of conditioning with animal training ("Sit! Good boy, here's your reward.") but forget that the same techniques are used on us all the time. Unfortunately, even if we don't know it, we are the mice in the box.

## Monkey See, Monkey Do

Giacomo Rizzolatti, a well-known neuroscientist of the 1980s and 90s, discovered a phenomenon that founded a new perspective on mimicking and modeling[5]. Studying the learning behaviors and neural responses of macaque monkeys in his lab, Rizzolatti found that neural activities of observed actions were recorded in the monkey's brains that were similar to the neurons later required to perform the action. In other words, he found that watching someone perform an action fires the same neurons in your brain as actually performing the action yourself. This then facilitates the learning process in that *mir-*

Monkeys, like humans, are social creatures that use each other to learn new tricks, skills, and techniques. By imitating each other, they avoid the more dangerous methods of trial and error.

*ror neurons* have already been fired before the action is attempted. This has been found to be especially effective in the learning of social behaviors through interpersonal relationships. Sequences of events, for instance, become acquired by observing the behaviors of others. By watching what others do, we think we know how to behave at a birthday party or at a job interview. Unfortunately, our ability to mimic the behaviors of others hinders our ability to naturally express our own behaviors. We then often find ourselves at a job interview pretending to be someone we're not in the attempt to impress while adhering to social rules.

## Social Cues, Social Qualms

Many people will think they are not so gullible. True. We're not all mindless sheep waiting to have propaganda inputted into our heads. What makes us select what we believe and what we reject stems from social learning. The Canadian psychologist Albert Bandura first realized that we could fully accept a model of behavior, fully reject it, or alter it based on our needs, interests, and abilities[6].

For instance, we learn how to solve problems by watching the way others do it. One model is to raise your voice, another is to keep calm and rational, another is to walk away, or mention it later along with all the other things you've been holding back. Where was your problem-solving model learned? How did you alter it to suit your personality and the contexts in which you may have to solve problems? We generally choose our problem-solving model based on whether or not it has worked, what kinds of rewards we obtained or forms of punishment we avoided, and the kinds of feelings the method prompted. Let's take the example of smoking and examine the forms of reinforcement that contribute to the habit:

- Direct social acceptance (I look self-confident with a cigarette in my hand)

- Indirect social acceptance (getting a smile from the person who's also smoking nearby)

- Environmental influences (smoking parents, friends, or colleagues)

- Peer pressure (everyone else smokes and if I don't they won't like me)

- Self-regulation (it's only a few cigarettes anyway)

- Self-reinforcement (I will gain weight if I stop smoking)

There are many positive models we have acquired by imitating the behaviors of others and reaping the rewards of social acceptance and approval (learning to speak and read body language, learning how to play an instrument or play a sport), but most of our behaviors are negative models. Knowing the difference requires coherence to your attitudes.

### Acting Under Hypnosis

Another form of social manipulation is the use of associations with certain appeals to urge desired behaviors. Selected information, disinformation, and distraction from the truth are exercised along with emotional pleas to persuade. In fact, that is the essence of propaganda: to influence the thoughts of a population by inducing an emotional rather than a rational response by discerning how the message is to be conveyed.

The fields of advertising, marketing, and sales regularly conduct expensive research to learn more about how to impregnate our minds with ideas, and have come up with an extensive list of strategies and techniques. Here are some of the most common:

- Argumentum ad nauseam: repeat, repeat, repeat!
- Ad hominem: attacking an opponent (their product is bad, buy ours instead)
- Joining the bandwagon: everyone else is doing it so you should too!
- Beauty: buy this product and you can look as good as the stars on TV!
- Flag waving: do it for your country
- Appeals to authority: if important people do it, so should you!
- Intentional vagueness: ignore fine print
- Guilt/compassion: what about those orphans?
- Fear: get this vaccine or you'll risk death!
- Promotions: free trials, rebates, coupons, etc.

Rest assured, the list goes on. When it comes to getting you to think a certain way or purchase unnecessary products, professionals know what they're doing.

## Passing the Mental Viruses

The word Memetics was coined by Richard Dawkins in his book *The Selfish Gene*[7] and was intended to constitute a mental parallel to the science of genetics. Memetics then evolved into a protoscience that studies the effect of imitation on behavior. Memes are units of cultural information like concepts, thoughts, habits, practices, terms, and other such influences that propagate themselves through people, families, communities, societies, and civilizations, just like genes are units of biological information.

Common examples include fashion styles, popular music, slang terms, health trends, religious beliefs, political ideologies, social rules, and so on. These are the man-made constructs that dictate what's right and what's wrong. We accept them as part of our culture and tradition and allow them to enter our lives to become the building blocks of our being. We hang on to brand names despite learning about how the product was manufactured, we rely on status symbols to inform us about people even when these symbols are inaccurate judgments, we cling to political platforms regardless of the wrong deeds the political members have done, and we won't let go of certain traditions no matter how obsolete and illogical they are.

Perhaps it's time to reflect on some of these ideas and think about what they really imply, whether or not they bring people together or drive people apart, what feelings they invoke, and whether or not any of it may seem just a little ridiculous to you.

### Why We Remain What We Are Not

Entire populations seem to live in a collective semiconscious Stockholm syndrome. They side with systems and governments that use forceful control and restrictions on them.

In his book, *Theory of the Leisure Class*[8], the economist and sociologist Thorstein Veblen explains that direct and indirect coercion are used to manipulate the population into maintaining social class divisions so that the leisure class can maintain control of their rank and use the arduous labor of the lower classes to their benefit. In Karl Lowenstein's book, *Governance of Rome*[9], examples are provided of wealthy people who maintained their political power in ancient Rome, by monopolizing land-ownership. The property-less proletarians had few options and little opportunity to resist their coercion in the light of weighted votes, legal jurisdiction, bureaucracy, corporate regimentation, and other such strategies. Try to operate through our modern Rome-like systems and you will see how controlling and halting bureaucracy can be. In the end, lower classes tend to turn against each other in their struggle to move above their current social status into levels of higher social power. Veblen suggests that one way the lower class members do this is by attempting to emulate their more respected counterparts in an attempt to gain higher social status through conspicuous consumption. Though Veblen focused mainly on anthropological examples of tribal behavior, little has changed in society today.

## Keeping up with the Joneses

The term *conspicuous consumption* was coined to describe lavish spending on unnecessary goods and services in an attempt to portray higher wealth and social status. The notion of class-consciousness is what drives people to reach for the dominant ideology of the times, eternally comparing themselves to people they look up to. Meanwhile, the power elites exploit this insecurity with market and media strategies that endlessly reconfirm imperfections and insecurities and encourage consumer behavior. Endless consumption to inspire envy from our acquaintances and temporarily boost one's self-esteem provides little more than immediate gratification and false expectations. Though evident, equating personal happiness with material possessions is an illusion many shoppers strive for.

Oniomania (being a shopaholic) is a condition that manifests with compulsive purchasing. Assuming you can forget your problems by buying brand-name items or thinking that expensive frivolity will make you feel ultimately better is an objectionable crutch. Even thinking that frugal buying with cheaper brands will help you cope with your feelings is a delusion that the market hounds use to increase sales and profits. However, those market hounds and sales experts will ensure they use all the techniques they know to influence you to wallow in your sorrows of dissatisfaction, low self-esteem, and materialistic fantasies. And if you think you're not so easily influenced, think again.

Neuromarketing, for instance, is now hitting the market strategies books. Using fMRI (Functional Magnetic Resonance Imaging) technology, neuroscientists have been studying memory, decision-making, and self-image as they relate to consumer behavior in the attempts to control purchase decisions. Movie trailers, car advertisements, erotic images, humor, and other methods to sway the audience have been studied extensively. But even beyond the recognition of new schemes, neuroplasticity (changes in brain structure) have also been studied in relation to consumer behavior. Soon, it will not be about whether or not you can be persuaded to buy a product, but whether or not you can be hardwired to be loyal to a brand or rewired to choose and publicly endorse one brand over another.

## You are Not a Standard

Though we often seek similarities with other people, we often forget that our strengths lie in our uniqueness. Our inner talents are like our finger prints, they are distinctive and specific. Our challenge in life is to decipher the print.

Even if not everyone has succumbed to addictive shopping or a false model of self-realization through money and fame, most of us have probably often believed some of the cultural beguilement used to create distraction from our true goals. The rationale behind equal rights, whether between gender, race, class, age, or sexual orientation, is a worthy and respectable cause, but those who would like to fight for these rights need to also understand that some objective differentiation needs to exist based on biological, and not social grounds. Not everyone wins in the Olympics. Not everyone is a mathematical genius. Not everyone can compose symphonies. No matter how many self-help books we read, we simply can't do anything we want to. This is false hope. We all have our special talents and abilities based on our biological makeup and should respect the indications of our skeletal, muscular, neurological, and creative selves.

*Your greatest strengths lie inside your specificity not in your equalization! Standardization is a terrible modern mistake. It is the tomb of self-expression, the eradication of traditions, and the end of personal freedom.*

The fact that everyone eats the same foods, watches the same movies, dresses the same way, and talks the same way is pure standardization, and YOU are not standard! You are unique. Your fingerprints, your voiceprint, your essence is different from everybody else. You are the Rosetta Stone you have to decipher and understand the world around you.

In the mean time, while society is focused on leveling the playing field so that everyone can get a ribbon just for participating in the games, the show goes on. Some unit (like a corporation, governing structure, or social organization) used surveys or statistical analyses to ensure the population is being leveled through standardization, ideological sameness, and homogeneity of desires. Media influences, chemical substances in our food and supplies, and low grade or ineffective medical, political, social, and educational institutions exist for that purpose: to make of you a dot in a statistical plot. It is not an easy job to rule countries and whoever does it is human and prone to mistakes. But do you want to be an effect of their mistakes? And who are "they"?

## Tunnel Vision, Tunneled Thought

You might think of your foe as a very vast and complex organism. It is in fact the sum of the conditioned conscious minds of entire populations. Your foe is the self-elected collective conscious that doesn't provide coordination and care for the system as a whole, but engages completely and secretly in persuading, influencing, and controlling the population in order to exploit it. When belief systems of these populations differ, their continuous struggle for self-affirmation results in conflict, thus causing wars, famines, and social destruction. Corporations and institutions are an enormous substantiation of the collective evolutionary glitch perpetrated by a false sense of reality, imposed chains of command, and social structures that function like endless mazes.

Just like a lab animal in the Skinner box, we are regularly habituated and sensitized to the problems of society. *Habituation* is disassociative programming used to reduce the intensity of what would be a natural reaction. An example can be seen in the use of alcohol. The first time a person drinks, only a few drinks will elicit negative reactions and intoxication. But when this person is habituated to the ingestion of alcohol, reactivity and recovery time are greatly reduced.

*Sensitization* has a similar connotation but with the intention of increasing reactions to stimuli. An example of sensitization is seen in one's reaction to a word, an image, or a topic associated with controversial content. While at first something may be considered funny in the style of a joke, or an interesting critical review, recurrent debate and in-depth focus on the issue will make one increasingly responsive to the content, frequently taking offense.

With years of exposure to various forms of socialization and media influences, we have become habituated to scenes of violence or stories of population manipulation and exploitation. Meanwhile, we have become sensitized to issues of race, gender, religion, and ideology. By focusing our attention on issues we are now sensitive to, we are distracted from, and pacified by, the powerful yet seemingly innocuous methods of control that are in place.

## When the Frog Croaks, it Rains

Many have not opened their eyes to the external influences controlling their lives and many who are aware have done little about it. The concept of the boiling frog provides a great example of what we regularly experience through social conditioning. If you place a frog directly into boiling water, it will react by jumping out of the pot. But if you place the frog comfortably in cool water, and gradually increase the temperature, the animal will not pay much attention to the increased heat and will slowly die.

*Please remember this very clearly*: Incremental changes and minuscule pieces of information or disinformation are easily left unnoticed or deliberately disregarded as inconsequential. However, the end result has immense implications. Movies, talk shows, music videos, and information learned in school and books are all small but constant pieces of information we come in contact with. Whereas information helps bring awareness to people, continuous and unremitting disinformation habituates and sensitizes the human conscious mind, much like a virus affects the body.

Alvin Gouldner, in his book *The Politics of the Mind*, refers to this fact:

*"What is needed is an understanding of how men act in countless ways to reproduce and maintain the very system that blocks their own liberation, and how this system is not only some*

*alienated thing apart from and rising above them, but is also rooted in their own daily doings, a myriad of mundane enactments countless tiny comings and goings.* "[10]

## *Viral Minds*

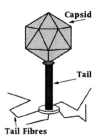

Capsid

Tail

Tail Fibres

Consider the following analogy:

A virus is a strand of genetic material covered by a protein shell called a capsid. The virus needs a cell to replicate and it uses its inner core (the nucleus) to activate the replication. Outside the cell, viruses exist as inactive and inert DNA or RNA. Just as a virus penetrates a cell to reach the nucleus and replicate itself with your DNA, a piece of wrong information (a wrong meme) can reach the core of your belief engine and use it to replicate itself. Like a virus, a negative meme can survive in the environment and wait for a core belief to be infected. Once infected, your core belief will act through contagion and will pass the same wrong ideology on to others. Like viruses, negative memes do not possess the power to self-replicate. They have to use the replicative apparatus from the host core belief that they infect.

For example, a meme could be the belief that black cats bring bad luck. This superstition cannot be passed onto others without being taught by a person (a parent, a teacher, a peer) or copied from a source (a written story, a symbol, a painting). Once the false notion is accepted, it is interpreted as truth and becomes difficult to eradicate. In fact, this person may even transfer the belief to other people who may pass it on again, and so on.

This is especially a concern for the more impressionable members of the population: the children. Media, education, and childrearing are among the most prominent methods used in western cultures to suppress natural and wholesome behaviors. This often occurs below the threshold of understanding, at a subconscious level, with more powerful and permanent effects.

We sometimes forget that common "education" on philosophical, psychological, and social topics addresses specific subjects over others, creates conformity to prescribed stan-

*"The direction in which
education starts a man
will determine his
future life."*
— *Plato*

dards of thought, and has a general tendency to indoctrinate with biased ideologies. Incomplete unsatisfactory education results in an incomplete unsatisfactory life. In our education, many of us have blindly memorized material for a test or written an essay by regurgitating the dictated material in the hopes of obtaining a good grade. The aim was not the information, nor the topic, nor the grade. The aim was to obtain acknowledgement. Our innate human tendency is to seek acknowledgement as confirmation of our value to society. Anything we are praised for leads us to consider ourselves worthy. If rewarded for an action we will tend to perform it again, even if it is not our favorite action or our tendency.

> *To repeat what others say is simple,
> to understand it requires wisdom.*

Social orders are equalizations or standardized statistical rules. They do not consider the best interests of the single person, but try to give a criterion and a model that keeps everybody within certain parameters. Ignoring your individual qualities will leave you incomplete. It is through years of conditioning that people have accepted to be ignorant of their true selves. Rather than questioning and investigating deeply the important issues that preside over our lives, many are content living in ignorance with incomplete or false information. If, however, we gain the awareness required to make the necessary changes in our lives, we can move forward to something bigger and better. Making the most of ourselves, achieving peak performances, and living a truly harmonious life will begin with a first step: *having the right attitude.*

## *Starting on the Right Foot*

### Separate from Conditioning

It would be a good idea to stop watching television, reading newspapers or magazines, or listening to the radio during the period you dedicate to reading this book. Separating yourself from information channels, in which you cannot carefully select the messages being conveyed, will help get you away from external sources of conditioning and allow you to focus more clearly on the guidelines presented in this book. In order to find your true life purpose, you will need to take the time to delve into your self and will need a clear mind to feel what you resonate with. If you take your mental and physical health seriously, and care for those you love, take regular time away from negative social influences of the media.

**Take Responsibility**

Everything we do comes with responsibility. Before you acknowledge that the right thing for you is to use your innate capacities to the best of your abilities, going against the hindrances society has purposefully imposed on you will only frustrate you. Before you start improving yourself, know that you have adversaries. These adversaries are institutions, written laws, and systems encouraging you to be what you are not. Highly structured, hierarchically controlled, and institutionalized, these adversaries create societies that are full of alienation and dehumanization.

**Consider Others Too**

Before you begin considering the self-challenge presented in this book, be aware of the external influences that try to dehumanize and generalize you. Consider this as well: when your progress is impeded, you are not the only one to lose focus. If you fall under social and personal pressure, those around you will be negatively influenced by your absence of direction. Think about the implication of your missed success on others. If you let self and social conditioning turn you into someone you're not, you are not the only one to suffer the consequences. To be true to yourself and follow your specificity is not only your right, it is your responsibility and your contribution to life.

"Responsibility does not only lie with the leaders of our countries or with those who have been appointed or elected to do a particular job. It lies with each of us individually."

— *His Holiness*
*The Dalai Lama*

# Chapter 3
# The Glitch

*"Success is going from failure
to failure without a loss of
enthusiasm."*
— *Winston Churchill*

Your body naturally serves as a compass that provides you with a unique orientation. As discussed in Chapter 2, you are constantly bombarded with influential messages that can derail you from your natural orientation and cause feelings of being lost and confused. Your body therefore reminds you of what you were born to do with natural inclinations and interests. The process of how to understand your inner core and find the future orientation that best suits you is not described until Chapter 7, because it is crucial to first understand that a mask or personality can smear your natural compass. This mask is formed as an evolutionary "glitch" in our nervous system. Not unlike what many psychologists have called the *ego structure*, a "mask" is a neural map imprinted in the nervous system by social conditioning, the same social habituation and sensitization discussed in the previous chapter.

A supportive environment that helps us to grow with the understanding of our natural tendencies and goals is the most ideal situation for optimal development. However, most people have encountered situations in which their natural way of being has been rejected. The social conditioning described in Chapter 2 can generate a sense of inadequacy, low self-esteem, doubt, anxiety, frustration, stress, and a myriad of other negative outcomes. This phenomenon is what we call *rejection* and can be seen in the forms of teasing, mockery, isolation from the social group, lack of appreciation or approval, lack of respect, feeling undervalued, or feeling ignored. Rejection generates internal disintegration of the personal core. Rejection is the opposite of a sense of belonging (Chapter 1) and kills the dream that a person has for his or her future. After feeling rejected, we find ourselves impelled to restructure our self-image to adapt and survive the demands of the environment. From that point on, our life becomes a compromise. This compromise generates a self-imposed personality that makes us become what we think we should be, not what we are.

## *The Mask*

Your "neural mask" is created in response to negative conditioning received in relation to the environment. Rejection causes compromise, which leads to the development of a *Persona*. The diagram on the following page is a model of how the Persona (from the Greek word *"persona"* meaning "mask") is composed of an extremely complex set of mechanisms. These automatic mechanisms will strive for existence within you, and will struggle to persist as collective ideologies or systems when operated on a larger social scale.

As early as the 8th century BC, wax tablets like this one were used as common writing tools. A *stylus*, a sharpened piece of wood, was used to engrave markings in the waxed layer.

In ancient Rome, Greece, and Egypt, scribes used to write using a wax tablet as their paper and a sharp engraving tool as their pen. Without coincidence, the Latin term for brain, "cerebrum," is literally translated into "made of wax." It was believed that the brain, at the early stage of development, is similar to a tablet covered in wax and it is engraved with furrows as information is accumulated. Though we are now aware that the brain is not an actual *"tabula rasa,"* scientific discoveries have come to the conclusion that furrows are "incised" by discharges of electricity and adrenaline. An intense electrical discharge is followed by adrenaline release, the shrinking of the brain's tiny arteries, and the formation of furrows in the brain. Neural connections and activated areas are visible with PET scans (Positron Emission Tomography) and indicate that the deeper they are, the more ingrained the information is.

Along the same line, experiences of social learning can also become incisions in the "wax" of our brains. As we endure moments of social programming, we become conditioned to restructure our personal nature into a personality that is more accepted by the larger group. The clash between one's personal nature and his or her environmental influences causes a sense of rejection or a state of *Anomie*. From the Greek *a-nomos*, mean-

## HOW A PERSONA OVERRIDES THE BODY

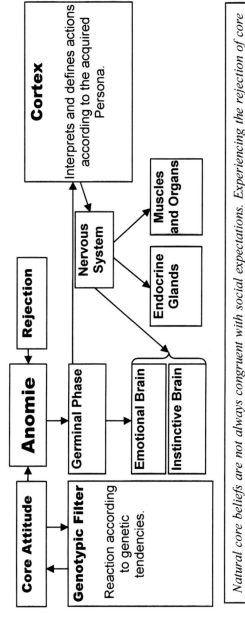

*Natural core beliefs are not always congruent with social expectations. Experiencing the rejection of core beliefs by influential figures leads to Anomie, the seed of a Persona. At the germinal phase where the Persona can grow in intensity, the emotive and instinctive parts of the brain become affected and weakened. When the nervous system and neural cortex are overridden by the Persona, the natural functions of other parts of the body are also affected.*

ing "lawlessness," Anomie is a state acquired <u>after</u> the cognition of being rejected. In this state, an individual feels literally ostracized, outcasted, degraded, and rejected.

## Anomie and the Broken Heart

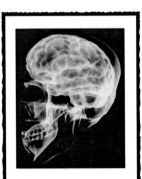

Recent research has shown that emotional impacts can mark the brain's surface. These impacts can drastically alter the way we think and act.

In the model proposed, Anomie can also be measured from its effects, one of the most interesting being the sudden decrease in the hormone Oxytocin. Oxytocin is associated with nurturing and social behaviors in mammals. This substance generates the behavior and the behavior generates the substance. Trust for others, social binding, social integration, relaxation, stress inhibition, tender affection, loving behavior towards children, generosity, warmth, and empathy are all fundamental qualities of a well-integrated individual and are all linked with this hormone. An acute and persistent drop in Oxytocin can be the sign of the initial state of Anomie. A similar state, a circumstance you have probably experienced at some time in your life, is also visible in the condition of the "broken heart." After a sentimental delusion or rejection the same phenomenon is presented and it is compensated with sadness, mistrustful behavior, withdrawal, and despair. In fact, Anomie is the exact opposite of falling in love and causes a sharp intense pain in the psychological core of an individual (especially in early development), often perceived in association with chest pain, a lack of social integration, increased fear, and an absence of trust.

Anomie acts as the epicenter of an earthquake in the brain, because of its intense emotional outburst. From there, something similar to fault lines can spread in all directions, causing mental blockages through learned convictions: a Persona is born. The Persona not only helps people deal with emotional pain but also acts like a mask that seeks acceptance from the

## PERSONAE FORMATION IN ORDER OF DEPTH

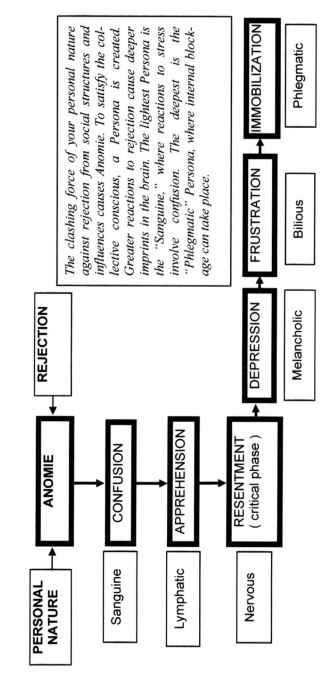

The clashing force of your personal nature against rejection from social structures and influences causes Anomie. To satisfy the collective conscious, a Persona is created. Greater reactions to rejection cause deeper imprints in the brain. The lightest Persona is the "Sanguine," where reactions to stress involve confusion. The deepest is the "Phlegmatic" Persona, where internal blockage can take place.

REJECTION

PERSONAL NATURE → ANOMIE → CONFUSION → APPREHENSION → RESENTMENT ( critical phase ) → DEPRESSION → FRUSTRATION → IMMOBILIZATION

Sanguine

Lymphatic

Nervous

Melancholic

Bilious

Phlegmatic

social system in which they live and grow. The Persona takes over our natural evolution and pulls the strings of our health and well-being in a very autonomic way. Unfortunately, this Persona becomes our conscious interface for our entire adult life, our hardened, prejudiced, and subjective defense mechanism: our alter ego.

### Getting Scarred

The thickness or intensity of the Persona varies according to the level of shock received. Intense shock or repeated impacts provoke circular and concentric furrows in the brain, like a scar. We therefore become "scarred" with experiences of rejection from the social systems and learn how to become what we are not. In turn, deeper furrows create a more ingrained Persona that becomes more difficult to change. In effect, the outcome of Professor Philip Zimbardo's *Lucifer Effect*, described in Chapter 2, is the Persona. Whether we repeatedly mirror the behavior of someone else, are repeatedly told that a certain way of being is correct, or have endured traumatic events, the furrows in our brain reflect the social conditioning we have adopted. An acquired personality is therefore a reconstruction of a new stand-alone, compromise-based entity. It is an unnatural neural map created on the basis of the rejection of one's true identity. The Persona hides your true essence, generating eternal dissatisfaction and blocking your evolution.

If we were to see the Persona as a mask we wear, the intensity of the emotional pain caused by rejection is proportional to the crystallization and the "thickness" of the mask adopted. A very prolonged, repeated, or intense pain or emotional trauma will cause a tougher mask so that less sensitivity to emotional or physical harm is achieved. In order to gain control over our environment, our Persona becomes a protective façade worn especially when meeting or confronting other people in social contexts.

As of the pre-teen years, the Persona activates in critical moments and instills doubt and negative self-talk, especially at times of integration with others. The habits then formed through repeated interactions with others become ingrained in our inner being, hiding who we really are from ourselves. Because it functions as a means of hiding the true self, the Persona is the root of any attempt of separation we perform in our life. The only alleviation from the Persona is to learn how to remove its structure and embrace the person underneath. The Persona holds the seed of resentment, thrives on fear, and dissuades you from trust and social integration. The Persona is a sociopath that functions as the trigger for all our psychosomatic disorders. Various medical conditions and symptoms are often masking a Persona's behavior. Any true, honest attempt to solve humanity's afflictions cannot disregard the mechanism of the Persona. The failure to recognize this condition can only lead to palliative solutions to deep-rooted suffering.

## The Fall of Man

This painting depicts Prometheus having his liver eaten  by an eagle. The painting is by Jacob Jordeans, 1640, and currently stands in the Wallraf-Richartz

The Ancients tried to explain the existence of a subconscious mind and warn people in many ways against the error of using the conscious mind as a guide instead of the subconscious. Ancient Greek mythology, for instance, held that humans once were immortal beings during a period of perfectly balanced existence adhering only to their subconscious. When the Titan Prometheus (whose symbolic name means *forethought* or *craftiness*) stole fire (conscious intelligence) from Zeus and gave it to the humans, the punishment was twofold. First, Prometheus was condemned to eternal sufferance by having his liver (the source of blood and thus the origin of life) eaten every day by an eagle. Secondly, humankind's acquisition of crafty misused intelligence caused the opening of Pandora's box, the root of all evil.

In this suggestive parallel, we can easily understand that

the Persona is not a modern disease. Many analogies have been made over the centuries to warn us of the misuse of the conscious mind. Entire Eastern belief systems were based on the separation from the illusory mind, called *Maya*. However, philosophies including Buddhism, Vedanta, and other belief systems failed to correct our descent into the structure of the conscious mind. *The defect of the self-formed Persona lies in the way our neural networks learn from the experiences of the environment. It is the inherent defect of our learning strategies; the Persona is the "Evolutionary Glitch."*

## *The Contaminated Mind*

With the use of the conscious mind and the continual acquisition of "rules of thought" as dictated by social constructs, the Persona becomes like a virus that can infect anyone, regardless of gender, race, and social stratum. As an analogy, a protein sheath of insulation naturally covers a cancer cell. The body does not properly identify the cell, because it is not considered alien and is thus protected by the immune system. In this case, eliminating the virus from the body becomes nearly impossible. When the inner core does not properly identify the Persona, the latter remains in the brain as an acquired conditioned neural map. The Persona can thus hijack the organism and act on our behalf, even if very mildly. Chapter 5 will explore the process to facilitate the re-adjustment of the internal state so that the Persona no longer takes control.

Therefore, when interacting with others, always remember that they have a Persona that is an alteration of the real being in front of you. It is a fake and unreliable entity that is prone to critique and negative behavior. When considering yourself, bear in mind that what you identify as YOU is probably a mixture of your innate tendencies and a strong influence of your acquired Persona. A Persona is NOT the real YOU, in the same way as a virus that infects you is a parasitic entity that lives inside you, and whose effects you express with various symptoms. A Persona is what is wrong in people. It is what hinders us to reach our full potential. If you ever wondered if there was anything wrong with you, you now know where to look for answers: it is the Persona. The discovery of the "Persona mechanism" is therefore a valuable advancement in human knowledge because it pinpoints the root of dysfunction in human beings. It is what lies at the base of racism, hatred, interpersonal dilemmas, social conflicts, unhappiness, and mental disease. In fact, it is in the Persona that mental illnesses, psychosomatic symptoms, and chronic ailments can originate. These Personae provide a template to understand psychosomatic illnesses, since the neural pathways of the brain are influenced by the Persona and directly affect behavior and neural function.

## The Brain Trap

The basic illness of the Persona is a schizoid temperament. A schizoid disposition is the tendency of the brain's neural networks to establish isolation and detachment from the various other cells that compose an organism. In other words, a mutiny between the brain cells and the body occurs so that the brain becomes overpowering and sabotages the physical functions of the body. Thus the brain builds its own trap. A Persona acts as an isolated entity that fears death and nullification. Once identified and counteracted, it will possibly react with anxiety or strategies to "survive" including panic, psychosomatic symptoms, confusion, and diversions. Every time you feel judgmental towards something, someone, or yourself, your Persona is fully active.

### Because the Persona is born of rejection, it learns to reject

At the very root of the Persona exists an "isolation" program. By distinguishing yourself from all those around you in a more or less competitive manner, the Persona separates you mentally so that you can no longer resonate with your environment. A Persona misleads your intuitions and redirects your thought patterns; it substitutes empathy with judgment and trust with suspicion. Therefore, by separating the brain from the body, the Persona limits your ability to understand the signs naturally provided to you that could lead you in the right directions. Essentially, the Persona is an infectious and contagious element that creates mayhem with the intent of controlling its host. Its contagious nature is what allows transmission to an individual that experiences rejection. Just like we can pick up a flu virus from people with whom we are in contact or from the environment in which we live, a Persona can be acquired through contagion. If a person is in contact with a specific kind of Persona while feeling rejected, it is very possible that a Persona-contagion might take place, similar to the memes discussed in Chapter 2.

## *The Formation of the Mask*

### From Rejection to Dysfunction

Though the intensity of the Persona can vary from individual to individual, its stages of development are common to all. The germinal phase of the Persona is a mix of depression, compromise, dissatisfaction, and latent quandary that harbors in the nervous structure of our brains. As it develops, with continuous influences from the social and ecological environments, it can greatly interfere with the body, to the point of changing the body's nuances and basic characteristics. *A Persona is therefore dysfunctional by definition and should not be accepted as a true representation of the self.* It is dysfunctional even for the body, since it will sabotage your health and well-being in order to obtain its agenda.

As mentioned, Personae are formed in response to rejection, reactive crises, or intrinsic strain. Depending on the intensity of shock associated with states of rejection, deeper furrows are formed in the brain and a tougher mask is acquired. Similar to defense mechanisms, Personae provide strategies to isolate from unwanted situations. In total, there are 6 types of Personae in relation to the neural formations. Each of these represents a gradient level of depth.

### Infecting the Mind and the Body

Because the Persona gets "engraved" as a neural map on the cortex, changes in neural activity directly affect the function and behavior of the body. For instance, in the left hemisphere, the area of the brain responsible for speech processing and sign production, and the area responsible for language comprehension and syntax are connected by a neural structure, called Arcuate Fasciculus, responsible for facial expressions. One can see

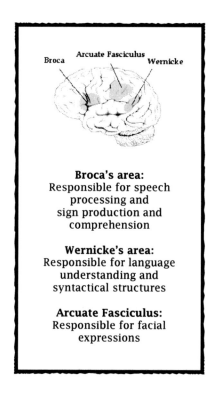

**Broca's area:**
Responsible for speech
processing and
sign production and
comprehension

**Wernicke's area:**
Responsible for language
understanding and
syntactical structures

**Arcuate Fasciculus:**
Responsible for facial
expressions

how stimulus from the Persona in these areas of the brain can alter one's behavior, expression, and manners of communication. The Persona literally becomes a facial mask that not only changes our forms of expression, but the facial features we use. In fact, the sensorimotor area of the brain, which is connected to all our body parts, is highly prone to changes in neural activity as related to Personae acquisition. Details on the effects on muscles, organs, glands, as well as metabolic and circulatory systems are beyond the scope of this book. Nevertheless, be aware that physical ailments can also arise from the use of Personae rather than the personal nature.

The following descriptions of Personae will not only allow you to identify where you stand on the gradient but also better understand those around you and the sources of your influence. When reading the description of the various typologies, remember that the Persona is like a noxious plant. It is cultivated from a seed; it can grow little or bloom fully, in accordance to the conditions that the environment provides. The six possible Personae described are portrayals of the fully "ripe" plants.

## Digging up the Roots

Looking for your Persona is identifying the parts of yourself that are at the root of your problems. It is extremely likely that while reading this section, strong feelings of rejection and discontent might arise. Be aware of this. If you start to become very judgmental, just make a note of it and carry on. The more your react, the more you know your Persona is being affected.

Because the descriptions outline the characteristics of <u>fully formed Personae</u>, they may accurately describe a fully developed Persona in you, or your characteristics may not be quite so intense because the seed of your Persona is still in its germination phase or already halted. Nevertheless, even the sign of the initial "virus-like" seed should be identified. If you think that you might have some defects, some emotional or psychological problems, or even physically vexing conditions, *start to look in the right direction; start to investigate your Persona to solve the root of your problems.*

If you have read through the Personae and find yourself having difficulties admitting that you have the seed of one of them, try to turn off your cognizant brain. The Persona does not want to be identified as a threat or as something you need to rid yourself of. It will try to generate doubt and disbelief for its own survival purposes. It may even try to push you into believing you have a different Persona than what you actually have in order to mislead you. Let your reactions guide you. If you feel personally affected or offended by the description of the Persona, that feeling is most likely elicited by the Persona in you.

If you can relate to more than one Persona, try to weigh them out so that you can identify the one you have in particular. Don't just think about the many contexts in which your character changes to meet social expectations, but think about the times your thinking processes block you from performing or achieving your goals. Although some people have more than one Persona throughout an entire lifetime, there is only one

---

**Are you still not sure? Ask yourself this:**

1. Have I got any significant problems or difficulties right        now in my life?
2. Have I had any significant problems or difficulties in the past?
3. Have I ever found the solution to my most persisting problems?

For those who like to be more pragmatic, take a piece of paper and write three major flaws, in very large capital letters, that you can identify in yourself. On a second sheet of paper, write some ideas about when and how you expressed each of these three flaws in three specific events. When you read through the descriptions of the Personae, see if these flaws get mentioned. You may be able to more easily identify the origin of these flaws while learning to be honest with yourself. Remember also that *you aren't the Persona, you ADOPT a Persona, and you can learn to remove the mask.*

that actually sits at the base of the problematic core at a time.

If you can successfully recognize your tendencies in one particular Persona, remember that admitting to its characteristics is not admitting your flaws. It is identifying the source of the misalignment and the sufferance you might bear, in order to finally solve your problems. Your cellular nature is essentially free of faults and you can learn to follow its drives and instincts. *Your Persona is not YOU!*

### Let Go of the Pearl

An oyster is a simple being, with a strong outer shell and a soft inner core. Sometimes, a small parasite or piece of dirt enters the shell and embeds itself in the soft inner core. Over the years, the mollusk will cover the irritating invasion with layers of nacre, creating what we know as a pearl. Though many people place great value on the pearl, it is nothing but a parasite to the oyster and yet, the oyster finds itself unable to rid itself of the pearl.

The Persona is very similar to this pearl. It embeds itself in the brain's neural structure and with time, it increases in size and strength. Even if it is currently small, it has the potential to grow. Though it may seem to increase in value and be loved by others, the Persona is still a foreign entity that does not belong and can even be harmful to the person who harbors it.

## Predicting the Storm Calls for Patience

Chapter 4 will clarify what some of the most typical reactions of the Personae will be and how to overcome the emotional challenges you may face. Chapter 5 will explain how to initiate a dismantling of the Persona's roots and how it "feels" to temporarily function without one. Rest assured that while reading the profiles of the Personae, a remedy exists and by the end of the book you will have a good understanding of the tools you need to obtain internal balance between your conscious and subconscious minds, thus readjusting your stance. Meanwhile, be patient throughout your readings.

When reading the following descriptions of the 6 Personae typologies, remember that the descriptions are portrayals of fully formed Personae and yours may not be quite as advanced.

The descriptions of the various Personae will include:

+ **Temperament:** A general description and outline of the Persona's "rules of thought"

+ **Interaction with Others:** Typical relations with others

+ **Gender Differences:** A brief comparison between males and females with this Persona

+ **Goals:** An outline of the underlying "program" used by the Persona to avoid extinction

+ **Effects on the Body:** The biological effects the Persona could have on your body

+ **Animal Analogy:** A simple analogy to more easily remember the Persona's main characteristics

+ **Probable Reaction:** The probable reaction of the Persona while reading its description

Understand that the cause of sufferance is the Persona and that the path to follow lies in the understanding of a clear mind, devoid of biased programming and conditioning. However, if you follow your Persona, you follow the same destiny that created it: a destiny of separation, quarrel, sabotage, and rejection. By following the Persona, you will comply with the little "voice" inside that pushes you towards the reiteration of bad decisions, self-sabotage, and error.

The 4 noble truths of Buddhism may help:

1.  Sufferance exists.

2.  There is a cause for sufferance.

3.  Cessation for this cause of sufferance is possible.

4.  There is a path to induce the cessation of sufferance.

# The Ephemeral

## *SANGUINE PERSONA:*
## *THE EPHEMERAL*

### Temperament

Sanguine Personae are formed by a superficial explosion-like phenomenon in the neural network causing tendencies of unpredictability, impulsiveness, and instability. This Persona is often associated with a bipolar manifestation of rapid alternated feelings of grandeur and hopelessness. People with this Persona might find it hard to persevere in any effort or activity that requires attention and determination because they are highly emotional, fickle, and easily distracted. Once the sense of novelty has passed, the Sanguine Persona finds itself quickly bored with repetition and incapable of continuing an enterprise.

I'm so bored! There's nothing to do!

Their ability to manifest mental complexity is limited to superficial topics that are not pragmatic in nature like acting, music, aesthetics, clothing, and other issues not vital for survival. Their fear of hard facts and their preference for indulgence in creativity leads them to often superimpose their own ideas and beliefs on what people communicate to them, breeding delusions and a false interpretation of reality. Likewise, they are communicative but not always patient. They can be animated and detailed in their expressions but often superficial and childish. With their attempt to prolong their discourse and be convincing, their explanations can be filled with trivial particulars that can often bore others in the conversation.

Creative and imaginative as well as childishly non-committing, superficial, irresponsible and self-indulgent, the Sanguine Persona is a very common model portrayed in the "Peter Pan Syndrome." Their hedonistic tendency focuses on having fun, enjoying new and exciting experiences, and participating in events where they can be socially stimulated. Any possible escape from an overly challenging reality combined with their naïvety makes them easily fall prey to party drugs, marijuana use, and other addictive habits. Food, alcohol, and drugs provide diversions from life's challenges and monotony and become tools for finding new social groups or to escape unwanted realities in life.

## Interaction with Others

Mobile, impressionable, and compliant, Sanguine Personae often manifest social warmth. Their eternal search for attention (both positive and negative) harnesses their eloquence and expressiveness. They find joy in being at the center of attention, and are ready to use any manipulative tool to get there. However, they can be credulous, naïve, and trusting and often overly sensitive to other people's judgment.

Sanguine Personae are ready to do anything to avoid solitude, monotony, and effort, three unbearable conditions to them. Generous and pleasant as company, they love to be seen as the social butterfly. Unfortunately for anyone who would like to be an exclusive friend, this Persona will often make you feel unappreciated, as though you are not a priority. Because nothing and no one is special for a Sanguine, a friend can feel like one of the many. Such a Persona is willing to have unstable and meaningless relationships or friendships to avoid being alone and to have opportunities to engage in novel experiences. Therefore, when something or someone bores them, they tend to craftily disappear from the scene and oscillate toward another newfound interest.

Similarly, people with Sanguine Personae remain superficial in their actions and always cast the impression that their energy is distributed, never concentrated. Not only do Sanguine Personae divide their attention to everyone around them, not giving precedence to those who deserve it, but they also perform actions in a puerile and distracted way. Their endless search for support and appreciation makes them easily lose the thread of an activity or discourse when confused about the ultimate purpose of their efforts. Especially when excited or under pressure, Sanguines will get confused about what they need to do and may use mischievous and immature strategies to avoid work. They go with the flow, led by the easiest route possible.

## Gender Differences

Males with Sanguine Personae have a tendency to live their lives regularly avoiding commitment because they fear that commitment, whether to a person, a job, or a responsibility, will result in their loss of freedom. Their need to avoid solitude generally results in avoiding commitment so that they can be freely involved with friends and activities for their personal pleasure.

Females with Sanguine Personae generally have such a strong need for social acceptance and attention that they can become manipulative, using people to meet their social needs. Women can be particularly affected by a sharp sense of solitude and neglect and might resort to using sexual seduction or pharmacological drugs or alcohol in the attempt to solve their sense of emptiness.

## Goals

Their goals are often trivial and fundamentally lacking in a sense of responsibility. During adolescence, Sanguine Personae find themselves more interested in social acceptance than direction and are often devoid of stimuli for their personal advancement or position in society. A major problem in Sanguine Personae is the lack of stable goals. This makes them jump from one experience to the other with peaks of excitement and misery that manifest cyclically. This simple adolescent style of thinking, with a focus on stimulation and social acceptance, continues throughout adulthood. People with Sanguine Personae are essentially continuously incapable of concentrating their attention and focusing on one target, often expressing a frustration with their goallessness.

Their tremendous lack of projection of their role in society keeps them from dedicating their full attention on tasks and goals of value. Their flawed external focus contributes to their tendency to evenly distribute energy on everything, making the most meaningful and the most trivial obtain the same amount of energy and attention. Because Sanguines attribute the same importance to everything, they are often indecisive and resort to decision-making through consensus. Unfortunately for them, they are generally incapable of discerning good sources of information and opinion.

### Effects on the Body

Sanguine Personae possess a "sanguine" temperament, associated with vascular and endocrine sensitivity. This is characterized by imbalances of the thyroid, and frequent periods of ups and downs in energy levels, in sugar levels, and metabolic activity. This can be reflected with frequent weight gain and loss, or water retention due to an alteration of the glycemic index. Similarly, their disorientation causes psychomotor and vascular instability, which are symptoms of their wavering energy.

### Animal Analogy

Imagine a dog, friendly, playful, and desperate for attention. They will do anything to maintain your interest in them, including learning tricks, obeying commands, and trying to use their pleasant demeanor to get the pats and treats they want. They hate being left alone and will participate in almost any activity rather than staying home. Their incessant desire to have attention and to please makes them the easiest of all species to train and control.

### Probable Reaction

When reading this description, the Sanguine Persona might become confused, anxious, disoriented, or simply deny the information presented. This Persona makes you think you are good as you are and you do not need improvement. Some Sanguines may think that they have a bit of all the Personae and are unsure of how to identify with a single one, so they may rely on consensus, asking others for their opinions. Others may accept that this is their Persona but might deny the intensity of the problem to justify the "rules of thought" of the Persona. They may think they work best as they do and don't want to consider changing. The Sanguine Persona survives by creating fog or uncertainty, or by denying the severity of the issue.

# The Grinding

# *LYMPHATIC PERSONA:*
# *THE GRINDING*

## Temperament

Lymphatic Personae are born from tree-like neural formations. They prefer unchallenging, peaceful, and quiet environments while disliking loud noises and chaos. This type of setting allows them to delve into an introverted state where they
can meditate or obsessively contemplate past experiences, current issues, and every possible future outcome. Their reflective
nature makes them slow and quite indecisive when it comes to
making decisions and taking action.

Unfortunately, this makes them also unable to act in times
of need. Just like a computer that slows down when too many
programs are being operated at once, the exaggerated analytical functions of the Lymphatic Persona can slow reactivity
down to a near halt. Not only are they masters of procrastination, but their endless mental computations and limited spon-
taneity can make them seem almost machine-like, eternally
losing the fleeting moments in life.

When faced with events that require excitement, energy,
and impulsiveness, they have no strategy and retire to their
internal world where they remain timid and emotionally closed.
Shy yet kind, the Lymphatic Personae appear delicate and will

become silent and withdrawn if offended. Nevertheless, beneath their gentle appearance, they generally operate myriads of mental processes and intense internal elaborations.

Because they believe everything can be assessed, classified, and sequenced, this analytical Persona could perform well in a lab, an office, or another controlled condition manufactured for complex mental activity. Unfortunately, life is not a lab. Sometimes events require momentum and acceleration. Imagine a person wanting to jump over a chasm. If he were to walk towards it at a slow and leisurely pace, he would never make it over the gap safely to the other side. Certain actions require promptness and cannot be taken gradually.

Lymphatics are prone to disorganization because of their multitasking habits, opening many files at once, working on all of them throughout different times of the day, and never putting things away. Their messy workspace or living space makes sense to them, because they know exactly where everything is, even if it appears chaotic to others.

All irrational and emotive behaviors are deemed unnecessary, unpleasant, and intolerable. The Lymphatic Persona is most commonly found in those who have no esteem for any lack of schematizations or anything that "goes with the flow." Lymphatics find human expressions often useless, vulgar, and unsophisticated. Chaotic or boisterous behavior and anything illogical or improvised is considered impossible to understand. Lymphatics therefore interact better with serene escapes to nature, computers, or libraries, rather than social groups or societies. Unfortunately, life is full of challenges and difficult moments that require reactivity, decisions, and zest. Their cold and detached observation of facts can be seen as sterile and removed from the reality of life.

They have a tendency to become addicted to the routines they establish, especially regarding food and exercise. Being very territorial, they like to know that they can easily retreat into a space of their own, where others are not welcome. This attitude can lead to Obsessive Compulsive Disorders where the process of repetition and introspection is so greatly magnified that actions cannot be performed in timely manners.

Rather than expressing their true emotions, Lymphatic

Personae tend to express passive-aggressive behaviors and bottle up their anger. Typical behaviors include stubbornness, procrastination, or constant failure to accomplish requested tasks. They may avoid direct conflict by leaving messages or by accumulating frustration that will manifest in sabotages. They will very seldom accept that their behavior is harmful to others, and when faced with this fact, they will respond with resistance and denial. This Persona thinks its behavior is appropriate because it is devoid of reactivity and does not understand that the build-up of anger mutates into obstructionism, sarcasm, and resentment.

### Interaction with Others

Their calm, cautious, and courteous poise allows them to adapt to social circumstances, as long as conflicts do not arise. Social interactions, to them, require extensive amounts of modesty and etiquette, with excessive sensitivity to confrontations and personal conflicts. Raised voices and intense provocations might be unbearable and frightening for a Lymphatic since they believe everything can be handled with logical and rational communication. Lymphatics can become even more quiet, introverted, and unemotional when hurt, challenged, irritated, or simply frustrated by their lack of readiness. They can stop communicating, refuse to answer to others, and choose to close into themselves. They can sulk, pout, or ruminate for weeks on the possible reaction or response they should have had at the time of confrontation. Not wanting to stand out, they therefore prefer to blend into the background where confrontations don't exist.

People with Lymphatic Personae are generally non-impulsive, hesitating, excessively self-controlled, and have difficulties integrating in new situations. Diplomatic and tolerant, they want to portray an image of restraint, poise, and class and will patiently wait for someone else to make the first move. Their wait-and-see attitude encourages them to mentally assess a situation and think about all the possible outcomes before deciding on an action. Still, they generally have a look that inspires dispersed calmness and approachability, with their meek and placid eyes. People may be inclined to initiate conversation with a Lymphatic only to realize that their apparent tolerance is instead a snobbish attitude towards others. Though Lymphatic Personae are never openly hostile, they have the tendency to condescend others in order to boost their own self-esteem, impress others, or to avoid quarrels.

Often firm believers of their own opinions, they can be tactless when exposed to other people, especially those who are emotionally expressive. Defensive, territorial, rational, and emotionally closed, they can react with detachment, particularly to those they don't know well. Just like they maintain self-control and show little passion or fervor for anything, they often fail to acknowledge other people's enthusiasm, energy, and spark. They can smother the fires in the hearts of their counterparts with their pessimistic caution to the point where it is almost unpleasant to be around them.

## Gender Differences

Both Males and Females with Lymphatic Personae tend to be slow and hesitant when facing decisions, but females will show their Persona in a more silent way. They will bottle up discomforts given by their hesitations, and will become gloomy and inactive as their frustrations add up. The need to avoid conflict keeps them from expressing their needs and feelings as they arise. Females tend to show they are upset by shutting down psychologically and physically.

Males with Lymphatic Personae can often be caught up in their obsessive thoughts, and become insensitive to their environment and its necessities. This can lead them to become untidy, shabby, and slovenly. Males tend to isolate themselves in their minds with their obsessive thinking, thus escaping the reality they have to face. To try to avoid conflict, they will first try to think about the best possible solution to the problem before openly discussing the situation at hand.

## Goals

Lymphatics are sometimes lazy and hard to stimulate into activity. They have difficulty beginning or initiating new activities because of their tendency to maintain habits and to see small challenges as overwhelming dilemmas to overcome. Their

tendency to "make a mountain out of a molehill" and to procrastinate so that they can find the time to mull over possible
outcomes makes their beginnings slow, doubtful, and unim-
pactful.

Lymphatics love sciences, technical innovations, and anything that imposes a configuration or a system to follow. However, their sensitivity to failure can make them easily lose their
drive. In addition to their knack to scrutinize over details, they
will find setbacks where there are none, or magnify problems
that would be easy to overcome for others. This can make them
easily fall into depression since they are unable to find creative
ways to solve their dilemmas in a timely manner.

Because they don't like a challenging environment, Lymphatics will tend to confine themselves in libraries, offices, or
private rooms, in search of a space in which distractions are
absent and they are free to flourish in their abundant mental
processes. Preferring philosophical hypotheses and scientific
theories, they will avoid chaotic environments. Some may
think that teaching is a good profession, only to later discover
that they have developed hearing loss and loss of vision in a
natural attempt to diminish the stimulation from loud rebellious students.

## Effects on the Body

Lymphatic personae are of "lymphatic" temperament,
with the tendency to suffer from ailments related to diminished
metabolic functions, impediments to $CO_2$ elimination, and a
low oxidative state due to lack of Oxygen intake. This might
also cause respiratory problems as well as fluid retention, con-
stipation, and weight gain.

Metabolic sluggishness is also a characteristic of the Lymphatic neural map, which is programmed to use energy spar-
ingly so that mental processes can take place. Lymphatics will
often complain about their frequent lack of energy and fall into
a state of victimization and discouragement for their lack of
vigor and sluggishness. Since the verve found in the get-up-and
-go attitude is seen as too demanding, their eternal struggle
with lack of dynamism sits at the base of their integration with
real life. They fail to realize that life demands heartiness, drive,

and promptness and often internalize their frustration in teeth grinding.

## Animal Analogy

Like cows, they will repeatedly and regularly ruminate over things they should have already digested. They are slow, and either stubborn or very docile. They do not like confrontation and would prefer being left alone for hours on end in their world of habits and routines. Although they are herd animals, cows like having their space to graze and will not interact much with others.

## Probable Reaction

The Lymphatic Persona has a delayed reaction and may read over the other Personae to make sure it has properly assessed each of them before coming to a final conclusion. It may not find a definite correspondence and it will use this "impossibility to generalize" as an excuse to dismiss what is presented as unreliable. This Persona is common in overly congruent individuals and it might take the time to reflect on the description before accepting it as pseudo-science, since the point is to strategically avoid any confrontation.

This Persona is commonly seen in scientific and academic environments. It has a self-opinion of poised judgment and rational congruence and a stubborn sense of quiet self-righteousness. It may even try to find the positive aspects in order to minimize self-criticism. Its procrastinated response could possibly set in motion a slow acceptance of the information read, with strong reserve and resulting in no desire get rid of it. Lymphatic Personae can experience excessive introversion, slow reaction to stimuli, detachment from physical and social activities, vivid imagination, social phobias, and timidity, all of which they justify with logic.

The Controlling

# *NERVOUS PERSONA:*
# *THE CONTROLLING*

## Temperament

Nervous Personae are born from a superficially rigid weave in the neural network. They are ambitious, independent, and highly driven to fulfill their self-imposed task, but are egotistic and un-empathic in their way of following their foals. They tend to do anything to reach their targets with unyielding determination. They tend to use their natural elegance in speech, decorum, and mannerisms to boost their success. Though they may not recognize how their treatment of others might be hurtful, they are sensitive to rejection and touchy about humiliation.

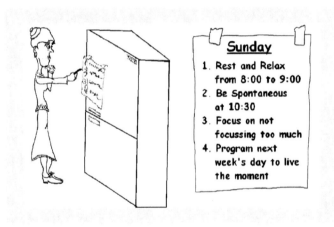

The most dangerous constituent of this Persona is the inconsiderate way they operate. Even if what they do causes others to suffer, they will find a logical rationale for their behavior. A model of the negative forms of this Persona can be found in any strict and ultra disciplinary regime or system where excessive control is forced onto others. Organizations that benefit from the misfortunes of others and legal institutions that are not always just are also examples of such behavior.

When raised in a loving and supportive environment, Nervous appear to be understanding and reliable. They will be devoted to their work to the smallest details, aiming for nothing less than perfection. However, they will always try to maintain emotional detachment from others so that their drive to work towards status or intellectual acknowledgement remains their priority, especially when they feel they are competing against others. Their drive for excellence makes them perceive the world as more challenging than it really is, causing them to feel like they are constantly working against the grain. Their main problem is their drive for perfection and intolerance to being controlled. They can easily learn rules of behavior from people of authority they respect and admire, but will adhere to those rules in such a rigid and inflexible way that they bury themselves into their self-made mental structures. This Persona does not work well with flexibility, contextual considerations, new contradictory information, or anything ambiguous.

Nervous possess an extreme sense of logic and order. They will be easily disturbed by illogical, non-sequential or anarchic thoughts and behaviors, often reacting with discomfort or agitation to social environments that are not regulated in accordance to etiquette and protocol. Their drive for personal success combined with their disinterest in others can sometimes isolate them from the social environment and even in their own families. Their proud and self-fulfilling ways make them sometimes avoid being part of frequent social gatherings because they feel the need to maintain a constant distance to focus on their self-consuming discipline. This can bring forth a state in which they lose the natural beauty of life, when they no longer stop to smell the roses, and become more bitter and stubborn in their Sisyphean life.

## Interaction with Others

Nervous are often found aiming for the peaks of achievement with a generally egoistic drive. These Personae often use conventional behavior and sentences to introduce themselves in a formal and slightly artificial way. This Persona will use exaggerated pronunciation and eloquent words to portray a perfect image of themselves that masks their internal anxiety for other people's judgment. People with this Persona will be sensitive to direct gaze and use a rigid posture, especially in the neck and spine, to emanate a sense of superiority to hide their self-critical tendencies or self-believed flaws. As firm believers of their logical doctrines, they tend to impose their pre-formed judgment on anything and anyone, can become strongly influential on other people, and present themselves as models, especially to young ones.

Though they are very critical of themselves, Nervous Personae are generally even more critical of others. They often choose positions where they think they can provide assistance through control, evaluations, or criticisms, but don't necessarily provide actual help. Seeing other people's inferiority helps Nervous perceive themselves in a better light. They therefore often crown themselves as judge and juror, critiquing others and thinking they can provide a flawless example. Unfortunately, they are more often unmerited and excessive. Though they may believe they are being harsh but fair, critical yet objective, they frequently find themselves debasing others. Especially when they feel that someone was cruel or unreasonable to them in the past, they will find retribution in being vindictive in return. Psychologically, Nervous Personae can suffer lethal blows if rejected and find it very hard to open up to emotions once hurt.

In social contexts, Nervous will often embellish their achievements, focus much of their discourse on current accomplishments and future opportunities for success, and will lie if necessary to portray the image they want. When people with Nervous Personae avoid revealing what they think, it is often because they suppose others either won't understand or won't agree, and can be a sign of their dislike for the company with whom the conversation is taking place. When they want to impress, they will focus on making good impressions by wearing the right clothes for the occasion, always looking paramount, and being on their best behavior. Conversations will flow around themselves or their occupation, paying little attention to others. They will also easily drop a friendship or relationship if an opportunity for higher prospects arises.

As parents, they will strive so hard for their children's perfection that they will unknowingly instill a sense of deficiency and inferiority. Because they will teach their children that everything must be flawless, they will not only make their children magnify their shame in the face of failure, but also provoke a desire to grow as independent individuals with an utmost mistrust for others. Nervous parents are generally poor examples of "family men" or "family women," teaching their children that love and romantic unions are not fundamental or even worth trusting, maintaining success as the priority.

## Gender Differences

Males with Nervous Personae will often be narcissistic and easily dissatisfied by the absence of perfection, even in a partner, and will strive to obtain the status symbols that will make them seem superior. They may tend to objectify women, maintaining a distant consideration, and preferring compliant companions. They are often attracted to seduction games that demonstrate their ability to dominate another, and may try to use their status, money, and lies to seduce one or more partners, only to reject them later.

Females with Nervous Personae will concentrate on developing an appearance of control and power, often imitating male behavior and showing off their equivalence or even supremacy over men. They will find partners with obvious flaws to justify their notion of superiority. Using mind games, sexual appeal, or other "controlling" behavior, they will try to gather experiences that reconfirm their strength, even if it means that they find themselves alone, believing no one else is worthy of them. Feminism is a powerful reactive meme, an offspring of the Nervous female Persona in response to male Nervous controlling behavior.

## Goals

Achievement is the only real goal in a Nervous "rule of thought" because it is the only objective of value a Nervous Personae sees. Control and status can prove they are better than, or superior over, others. They may, for instance, use work and intense self-discipline to succeed and occupy high places in society. The Nervous love for order and establishment is always strong, even if it's not very visible or carefully well hidden. Sometimes they use the façade of a wise advisor, when they actually want to place boundaries on the freedom of others through tests, evaluations, and protocols. They want others to prove themselves according to the Nervous standard ("I'll accept you if you can prove that you're like me").

Nervous, therefore, enjoy positions of authority, where they have the ability to influence others, or where others are forced to look up to them. They want to receive respect, controlled conditions, and logical order. Because their biggest flaw is their lack of consideration for people, it is unfortunate for the rest of society that they are often found in places of high social status, like academia, business, medical professions, law, and government organizations. Actions like creating and installing laws, regimenting professions, controlling others and their work, institutionalizing activities, imposing sanctions, or promoting religious dogmas and doctrines are perceived as necessary to ensure the collective Nervous Persona's survival. The focus is on personal success and power, which is demanded both in the workplace and at home.

Nervous Personae always need to know in advance what is going to happen, they love to program their activities, and they detest unexpected events. Schemata and logic are essential and everything that is chaotic, emotional, or uncertain is carefully pushed away as it is seen as destabilizing. Although Nervous Personae might act as a social constraint mechanisms for other people, they will hide their own personal flaws through lies and secrecy. They thus seek isolation for themselves while trying to impose individualism and order onto others.

### Effects on the Body

Nervous Personae have a "nervous" temperament with a tendency to suffer from ailments of the nervous system and calcium malabsorption. Their obsession with order, protocol, and decorum can become neurotic to the point that they obsess over minor details. Their fear of failure, imperfections in their work, or blemishes in their appearance can magnify to the extent of paranoia. Furthermore, their mistrust and suspicion of others, sometimes a reflection of their own untrustworthiness, can influence the metabolism of calcium and create a condition known as "calcium shell," characterized by calcium deposits in tendons and muscles. This causes stiffening in the muscles and joints as well as in the cranium, where convictions can be fossilized so that nothing can change their mind. They are therefore prone to arthritis, arthrosis, and other ailments that cause stiffening and pains in the skeletal structure.

## Animal Analogy

Horses like to perform but accept control only after careful training. They frequently play games to determine which one dominates and then respect the hierarchy created. It takes a lot of energy, patience, and understanding to work with a horse because of its innate tendency to be over-sensitive, to maintain a chain of command, to be dominant, and to ostracize anyone they don't like from the herd.

## Probable Reaction

The Nervous Persona, when presented with the full effects of its behavior, will first pretend to ponder over the concepts when actually trying to come up with ideas to discredit them. They will be highly skeptical and will try to find the origin of the sources. Even before trying to understand, they will want to know the source of information, see if the background has been accepted by accredited sources, and if enough "proof" can support the ideas. They will judge the language used, the writing style, the references, the quotations, and every note that can delimit the "status" of the source. They will be skeptical about the source of information, relying solely on previous rank, category, and class to be the judge of credibility. When the Nervous Persona is at its full strength, it can cause states of paranoia, rigidity, hyper criticism, suspiciousness, over controlling habits, and a desire to dominate other people.

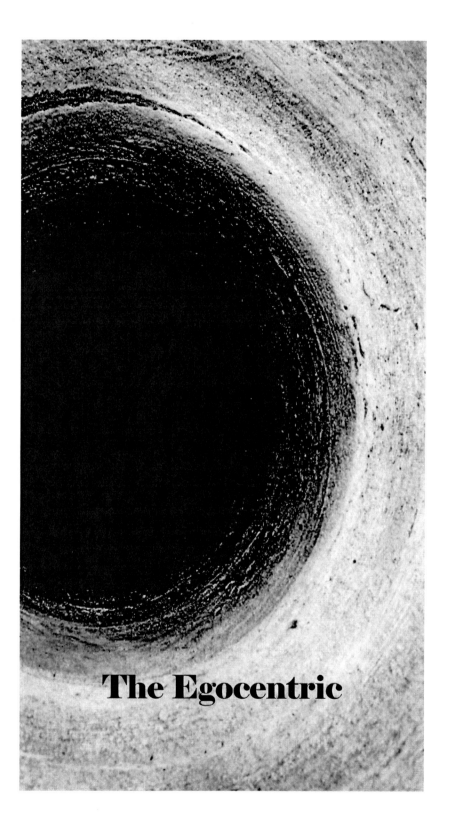

The Egocentric

# *THE EGOCENTRIC:*
# *THE MELANCHOLIC PERSONA*

## Temperament

The Melancholic Persona is born of a deeper concentric and centripetal neural structure. Their way of thinking becomes self-reflexive, a self-contemplative, hypersensitive, cautious, and Machiavellian. Though they may seem warm, friendly, and open, they can also be quite cold, introverted, and highly self-centered. They are essentially vulnerable and sensitive, in addition to having very low energy levels. They will therefore focus their energy on themselves and on obtaining what they want and need from others. Being more theoretical than pragmatic, and devoid of a strict moral code, Melancholics easily become astute manipulators of others, learning to rely on people and environments to limit their energy outputs. The weak, gloomy, and pensive temperament of Melancholic Personae makes them easily disheartened and apathetic.

People with Melancholic Personae will often perform with bursts of energy, followed by extreme or lengthy moments of fatigue. Preferring philosophical examinations of existence and deep introspection, people with this Persona are often involved i n

but I thought I was the center of the universe!

meditation, new age thoughts, and ethereal forms of expression. Their passivity, solidarity, and depth of thought, combined with their dreamy and distractive mind, makes them great developers and interpreters of symbology, art, poetry, and other forms of ambiguous expressions. In fact, in ambiguity lies the Persona's strategy. This Persona does not like things that can be clearly proven or explained because it thrives on the confusion that deeply philosophical conversations can create.

Religious tendencies, as an attempt to find refuge from a hostile world, are very common for the Melancholic Personae. Traumatic events often result in states of mania, depression, self-harm, and melancholia. Sometimes, Melancholics express their absence of energy and desire to escape the world through non-sequential utterances, ideas, self-talk, visions of religious icons, and hallucinations. Escape from the social environment is seen as a way to denounce their resentment for perceived misgivings.

Melancholics can be envious, dark, and seek drama to exorcise their internal problems. They are warm and fluent in words but cold and withdrawn at heart, and possess a fleeing, non-confronting gaze. Melancholic Personae generally feel vulnerable and exposed in situations they can't control. To counter their inner fears, they will show a confident and laid-back appearance. When faced with too much difficulty, the Melancholic survival technique is to use escape, victimization, depression, or illness.

Often afflicted by anxiety and introspection, they can be easily frightened. Fear can make people with the Melancholic Persona freeze and can even induce internal tremors or fainting. Anxiety can manifest as barely perceptible movements such as rhythmical suction of the lips (very similar to the suction of an infant) or a scouring movement of the hands (which recalls the soothing effect of the mother's skin).

At the most intense level, Melancholic Personae can become slightly psychotic and function in a reality made of past traumas and fears that have not been completely surmounted. The external world is perceived as unsafe and intimidating. The search for protection becomes a central drive in this Persona.

The neural network attempts to reconfirm the belief that they are not loved by using states of disease to get attention in a very indirect way. Self-harming behaviors are used to justify the inability to work or perform while obtaining support from others. Anorexia or bulimia, skin-picking or cutting, hair pulling, and any form of self-inflicted damage with the clear intent to do so is activated by this Persona as defense mechanism.

## Interaction with Others

Envious and easily resentful, Melancholics use weakness as a strategy to attract attention. They work like spiders, using hypnotic and spellbinding moves, words, and intonations to weave a web that is apparently very weak and almost invisible but is actually quite resistant. They attract the people that want to help and will do anything to try and keep them trapped in their web. Masters of "being hard to catch," Melancholics are often ephemeral and phantom-like in their personal commitment to others. These Personae express a profound sense of egoism that acts like a black hole for other people. Often showing symptoms of primadonnas, they will open up enough for others to enter their realm only to close again, leaving helpers confused yet willing to try harder.

Melancholics possess a sinuous, spooling, and mesmerizing way of interacting and surviving off others. The Melancholic Persona, when strong, is often incapable of providing sincere love because "the rule of thought" is that they should be taken care of and they deserve protection and shelter. They are greedy for attention and care but not ready to exchange equally with mutual affection, reflecting the selfish, infantile approach that takes everything from its source of sustenance.

This Persona therefore often searches for paternal or maternal figures to use as economical, emotional, and energetic support. After they have lived off as much support as possible from their family, they will find someone else to support them, using various strategies to elicit compassion and kindness from others.

Extremely clever and imitative, the Melancholic Persona uses social camouflage to play a desired role and thus appears extremely different from what is inside. Underneath their outer shell, people with this Persona are unforgiving and indirect, finding pleasure in influencing their supporting figures  by expressing dependence. Astute observers, they enjoy the control they have on other people's emotional fluctuations. Their ability to think in complex ways with their mental flexibility makes them good learners and analyzers that can manipulate others' emotions. The Melancholic Personae will find the most opportune moments to fall ill or weak so that others' possibly waning attention gets refocused onto them. With their spiritual and loving façade that hides their innate fear of confrontation and combat, they will find refuge in conditions where they feel protected.

In addition to their chronic reliance on others without exchange, Melancholic Personae often refer to religious idols or divinities in search for metaphysical protection. Because they feel weak when they are alone, they are helped by the thought that a spiritual being that is looking out for and protect them. Though they may not admit it, the Persona is too weak to survive on its own and is strengthened by an external source of energy, whether spiritual (through religion) or physical (in someone else).

When not in a relationship, people with this Persona can become deeply melancholic and burdened with dark emotions. They can manifest gloomy, moody, and anxious states as well as frustration and interest in "self-help" techniques or psychoanalyses. Sometimes they can reach the point of becoming hypochondriacs, desperately searching for any kind of help and support, even from professionals. Melancholic Personae are characterized by a condition of fear and an internal lack of strength. People with such Personae resort to mental influences to obtain what they desire and employ ambiguity to confuse the people who ask for explanations.

When raised with love, Melancholics can grow with the confidence that gives them profundity, but not a daring attitude to take on the challenges of life. When devoid of energy or when raised with little affection, they will often fall prey to psychotic breakdowns. They will then try to get attention from helping figures like doctors, psychologists, specialists, tarot card readers, and priests.

## Gender Differences

When female, the Persona will use feminine forms of appeal to seduce a provider and to keep the partner hooked. They will use physical illnesses, weakness, and psychotic breakdowns to portray a constant need of the other. Once they have obtained someone's attention, they will hysterically play subtle mind games, generating an emotive dependence.

When male, the Persona will be oriented to being a sensitive "lover," relying on the practice of poetry, dance, music, and other creative arts, or simply a very unimposing appearance, to represent a person who is in tune with his feminine side. Unfortunately, they will find very little satisfaction in strong, healthy, and loving relationships, and are often unreliable partners. Slightly weak and unable to support themselves completely, they may also resort into financial, emotive, and psychological support from their partners.

## Goals

Melancholic Personae often try to compensate for their vulnerability by studying psychology, meditation, or other practices that are meant to heal the mind. They sometimes study the psyche to the point of feeling lost, confused, and profoundly insecure. This Persona maintains a distance from the strong, lively, animal side of the human being that allows physical stamina and work. They often want to be seen as "masters," "gurus," or inspired philosophical teachers, and use languages, dresses, and scents that can be seductive. As a simple rule remember that "if its vague, it's Melancholic". Therefore, languages, religious, and new age doctrines, poetry, refined artistic expressions, and anything that would require no adhesion to physical proof fascinates them.

## Effects on the Body

Melancholic Personae possess a "melancholic" temperament that creates a constant influence on the adrenal functions (glands that release stimulating hormones located above the kidneys). Adrenal shutdown is a reaction to the Fight or Flight response mechanism with a distinct predominance on Flight and parasympathetic activation. This Persona has a strong influence on the body's energetic output and creates a state of constant frailty. There is therefore an expression of strong interest in health issues, natural foods, spiritual topics, psychology, and self-help because they are generally lacking in these aspects.

The Melancholic neural map also impacts the digestive system by slowing down the metabolism of proteins that results in an accumulation of indole. This is a precursor of increased serotonin (5HTP) in the brain, which creates a self-produced hallucinogenic state and a feminine side that appears sophisticated, seductive, unthreatening and charming.

Anorexia and bulimia also stem from the Melancholic Personae and are much more common in girls than boys. Melancholic Personae in boys would instead manifest through effeminate or sophisticated behavior. To this Persona, suffering is not only part of life but is also a tool of domination, manipulation, or revenge. When needing support and sustenance from others, or when expressing intense resentment towards a parental figure, Melancholics can be extremely unforgiving and will often wait for an appropriate time to draw the attention of others back onto themselves.

## Animal Analogy

 The Melancholic Persona is like a snake. It is shy and it survives by hiding or through quick retaliation from unwanted situations. Being ectothermic, snakes depend on the warmth from their environment to survive. Though they can have bursts of energy to capture a prey, they often need their time and space in isolation to acquire sufficient thermal and energetic equilibrium. They are flexible and can blend with their environment, not wanting to stand out from their protective shelter; but cross their path and they will bite. It is a good habit never to underestimate the retaliation capability of Melancholic Personae.

## Probable Reaction

While reading about its own Persona, the Melancholic will

probably find the information preposterous because their self-perception is that of a spiritual and caring being. They will deny the information read completely or try to identify with the less individualistic model proposed. Thinking that it is full of love, the Persona will find it ridiculous to imagine that it has a manipulative or even resentful tendency to gain emotional and psychological control over others. It will manifest resentment and incredulity towards the source of information. It will feel exposed and it might react with signs of stress such as smoking, nail biting, or altered breathing.

# The Rebelling

# THE REBELLING:
# THE BILIOUS PERSONA

## Temperament

The Bilious Persona is created by a deep fracture-like incision in the neural network. It is associated with reactivity and open challenges with a behavior is normally direct, impactful, disordered, and certainly not diplomatic or reserved in any way. They can have animated facial expressions, piercing or challenging gazes, and strength in their movements. They are rarely at ease, often feeling the need to move, and need constant stimulation. Impatient, hyperactive, impulsive, and combative, they show their passion in impetuous ways, without necessarily intending to. Their internal chaos pushes them to follow many projects with great enthusiasm, but seldom to conclusion. They are self-confident and enjoy challenging themselves and others through mentally, emotionally, and physically competitive means.

Generally, Bilious Personae are hyperactive, animated, and enthusiastic but are also easily irritated, short-tempered, and incapable of compromise. People with this Persona are able to push themselves to the limits, exceeding in anything they want with zestful energy, and will move beyond stability to reach new stimulation. Naturally competitive, they will often try to be right. When being "right" is a main objective, they will go far to prove this point even if it is only to prove the other "wrong." In fact, because the core of this mechanism is

"I am right, you are wrong," even when others are trying to agree with them, Bilious will regularly find someone or something to blame.

Unable to admit their faults, Bilious Personae relentlessly want to win, both physically and verbally. In the case of the latter, they often lack serious arguments, and may result to false recollections of events to justify their point. The Bilious neural network is programmed to prove itself right, not to remember the real facts so it may even remember events erroneously and then believe them to be true. When presented with a truthful reality, they may be unable to conceptualize it or become irritated and dominate the scene with a tantrum. Such Personae are therefore intolerant of other ideologies, thinking that their way is the only right way, and may try to impose their personal view on others. What they have learned and accepted will become unchangeable rules that they will apply to everything and anything, even when it is inappropriate or illogical. They do not always care about what is practical and logical, just what they think is right.

During early adolescence, Bilious can only learn through practical examples and can't stand theoretical explanations. They dread immobility and inactivity behind a desk because they feel the constant need to unload physical tension through sports or competitive activities. Being prohibited or inhibited in their movement is a horrible punishment to this Persona. If there is no activity, the Bilious will lose interest, fall asleep, or be unable to pay attention. Should that fail, they may resort to initiating disorder and turmoil to avoid the imposition of immobility. Sometimes rebellious activity is used to express the frustration and irritation of too many rules and constraints, resulting in vandalism, attacks to the community, and noise creation.

When not physically competitive, Bilious Personae can be studious but intense critics of people and systems. They will attack, with full rage, any ideological imposition and can become blasphemous, offensive, rude, and vulgar. They may use their high reactivity to generate reactions in others or try to make a scene, as though they could prove their point with noise and chaos.

The Bilious purpose is to generate destructive interference to shake things up because fights and arguments represent a dynamism they believe is essential to express life's vitality. Natural momentums created with peaceful discourse are too boring for them.

Fundamentalist cultures tend to reflect some of the expressions of the Bilious Persona. Their deep and totalistic commitment to their beliefs, which they try to impose on others, can result in confrontation and conflicts because they refuse any opposing arguments, even when supported by evidence.

## Interaction with Others

The Bilious Persona doesn't have a problem with people telling them *what* to do but *how* to do it. They are naturally rebellious against timings, methodology, and any imposed process or system. They do not like order, protocol, or codes of behavior and will see any such imposition as a dare to defy. Bilious are stimulated by challenge and will engage in tasks with great enthusiasm, but often overestimate their capabilities and resources. They often appear to be overconfident, arrogant, and proud, and will act impulsively with vigor and no tactful adaptation to the environment. Their actions can become so inappropriate that they can cause more damage than good, especially when they speak. They like to express themselves and their stubborn convictions with uncompromising and unidirectional thoughts, even when not asked or when undesired. Their offensive manner is frequently insensitive, hurtful, and can initiate fights.

Initially, the Bilious Persona is very social, but is expressed with a lack of etiquette, a diminished interpersonal space, slightly invasive manners, and crude jokes or inappropriate conversations. They are vivacious and sharp but highly insensitive to the signals they receive from others. Their desire to perform their best and regularly impress makes them internally maintain high standards of themselves, but advice and suggestions for improvement are perceived as something to fight against. Solutions to problems are frequently binary, an "all or nothing" approach that is unable to perceive the middle ground. Furthermore, when advice is given to a Bilious, it is often seen as a challenge to prove wrong and will encourage them to act in the opposite way of what was advised. They will not respond to talk or reason but must interact through confrontation, where only the strongest conviction, not the most logical, can survive.

While they do not take criticism well, Bilious do like attacking others for their errors and flaws. They do not like to see weakness in others and can callously pass judgment with sarcasm and little sympathy. Because they like challenges, they may want to drive others into confrontation by pushing buttons as well as creating upheaval. Slowness or hesitation can unleash fury and rage in a Bilious Persona. Even strolling at a slow pace or being behind a slow car will seem like a limitation to their personal freedom. Anything perceived as quiet and modest feels lifeless. They need to move, make noise, and cause chaos.

Belligerent and easily bad tempered, they are often in a rush and they use the same hasty critical process to jump to conclusions and impose these on others. Often these conclusions are little more than reconfirmations of their own convictions. Errors in judgment are common for this Persona, especially when considering other people and the differences in all of them. Because they are not tactful, diplomatic, and sensitive, they are often unable to consider nuances and individual differences.

## Gender Differences

Males with Bilious Personae are generally simple, direct, and abrupt. They will often pick the taboos of a group and use them to push people's buttons in order to initiate a negative response. They perceive a conflict situation to be more interesting than other forms of communication. Their desire to shake things up also makes them often oriented towards adventurous and dangerous activities.

Females with Bilious Personae need lots of movement and physical activity. They show their rebellious side with a masculine touch, becoming tomboys and challenging males in verbal or physical confrontations. When they find themselves in situations they don't like, they will often complain about their problems as though they were caused by somebody or something else, and are unable to be convinced to accept their mistakes.

## Goals

Bilious put all their attention on proving themselves. They like to prove themselves right, strong, and fast, and therefore prove others wrong while being intolerant to anything weak or slow. Because everything is seen as a competitive game, they want to break the rules and push the barriers. They are rebellious in nature and like to be provocative. Strong reactions, to the Bilious Persona, mean dynamism and liveliness. They are not good leaders because they can collapse a group with their personal fights and fits of temper. Nevertheless, they can become good executors of clear and concise tasks.

## Effects on the Body

Bilious Personae have a "bilious" temperament with a tendency to suffer from ailments related to an intolerance to external stimuli and an altered production of bile (a fluid stored in the gall bladder used to digest lipids). This can cause altered blood reactivity and hormonal imbalances that develop symptoms like nausea, gastric pains, migraines, insomnia, agitation, food and environmental allergies, and other symptoms.

As children, Bilious Personae might suffer from dyslexia, ADHD, or a strong lack of focus. The Bilious neural map can activate liver failures, which would result in Ketosis, an accumulation of excessive acids in the blood and therefore an "acid" behavior, and commonly auto immune diseases.

## Animal Analogy

You might think of a Bilious as a wild cat. Signs of weakness will push them to engage to fight to overcome their prey. They must regularly prove their strength and vitality to claim their territory. They are abrupt, reactive, stubborn, and naturally aggressive. They attack weakness.

**Probable Reaction**

The Bilious Persona will first react with a "no" attitude. It will start by being argumentative, turning to someone else to express its disagreement on the style this book is written, the author, the topic that seems absurd, or any possible subject to impose a negative comment upon. Strong negative comments might arise. Belittling and demeaning of the description of the Persona and maybe a sense of frustration and rage might follow the initial sarcastic response. After prompting to put the book away for a while, the Persona might become irritated by the messages read and come back to the challenge, possibly a challenge to prove the source wrong.

The Minimalist

## *PHLEGMATIC PERSONA:*
## *THE MINIMALIST*

### Temperament

Phlegmatic Personae are born from deep, amorphous, and dense grooves in the neural network. Passive and economizing, Phlegmatics avoid waste as much as possible. They prefer to stay where they are and maintain what they have rather than struggle for something better. Once they have acquired their basic needs of food, shelter, and a partner, they become content and strive for little more. Afraid of the unknown, they like to be on stable ground with people they know and in a comfortable routine, placing a strong importance only on defending their possessions, their property, and their land.

Slow entrepreneurs and business operators, they concentrate on avoiding loss rather than procuring gain. They can become obsessed with saving money or resources and will tend to re-use what they have, becoming misers who won't throw anything away that may save them a penny in the future. Rather than buying new items or appropriate materials to fix items, they will creatively solve problems with the simple materials they already have.

The Phlegmatic Persona will, however, often manifest some materialistic obsessions and find pride in being able to show others its new belongings. Whether it be plate collections, new gadgets, brand-name clothing, or cars, people with this Persona will frequently spend money on their desired objects, sometimes neglecting other more important areas that require financial attention.

People with a Phlegmatic Persona will also establish a sort of security and spirit by enduring hardship, engaging in activities of prolonged physical stamina, and plunging themselves in natural settings. The Phlegmatic Persona is attracted to essentialism, pragmatism, and the spirit of survival. It does not have a high regard for intellectual activity, particularly anything theoretical or philosophical. People with this Persona have no care for order, protocol, or paperwork and, rather than theorizing about outcomes, they need to apply new ideas in the most life-like situation possible. Because of their lack of discipline, new activities are soon abandoned due to a lack of interest or lack of desire for improvement.

Mentally slow, calm, and moderate, people with a Phlegmatic Persona are unable to be productive when not motivated to work. They like to work only when it's time to work, generally move at their own pace, and feel the need to indulge in mindless activities (like watching television, sleeping, or eating) to rest. By attending to their primary drives of eating and sleeping, they take their time to replenish their energy level but they do not like to expend energy when it is not needed, especially emotional expressiveness, communication, lively gestures, or animated facial features.

Life is normally perceived as a period to enjoy sensual pleasures and everything else might become an encumbrance. Their houses and their way of living are maintained with the bare minimum essentials, without aesthetic or artistic architectural features. For those with a Phlegmatic Persona, only the most necessary is required, the rest being simply a waste of resources, money, and activity.

The Phlegmatic pragmatic approach is oriented toward using the least amount of effort possible. Their enjoyment of passive activities, such as watching TV, when combined with their regular needs for food and rest, can result in weight gain. They do not like physical activity beyond a certain point, and need absolute lethargy to balance their energy outputs. The Phlegmatic Persona fears mobility and territorial changes, and would much rather stay stable while limiting frequent movements and exposure to novelty.

### Interaction with Others

This Persona likes to stick with what it knows. It does not like novelty, innovation, or change in lifestyle. Before trusting a new idea, people with this Persona will need to try it out for themselves, as long as it doesn't require too much effort. It is for this reason that they generally feel uncomfortable with anyone who is different from them. Though the Phlegmatic Persona can be friendly and kind, it is usually introverted and reserved. They like to remain within their comfort zone, do not approach new people very often, and do not always look approachable. They have, however, a general comfort with natural environments, being kinesthetic (sensorial) in nature.

Strong and unemotional, the Phlegmatic Persona is stubborn, territorial, and quite insensitive. Uncommunicativeness, inertia, emotional numbness, and indolence are common traits. People with a Phlegmatic Persona are generally not people-friendly. However, since this Persona understands the environment through the senses, what is most pragmatic is better understood. Working with building materials, industries, farms and fields, animals and wildlife, their general approach is to make use of what is available. Unfortunately, sometimes this is done with no forethought, exploiting natural resources for maximal gain. Due to a basic indifference and resistance to hurtful stimuli coupled with a lack of remorse, this Persona can perform actions that would be deemed traumatic for others.

This Persona survives and gets transmitted better in rural communities. Though they can endure physical labor, unpleasant environments, and mindless repetition, they are also capable of performing actions that sensitive people abhor. In addition, due to a lack of mental flexibility, there is a difficulty understanding why others do not think or act similarly to themselves.

Without a definite moral code or a sense of guilt, the Phlegmatic Persona can easily behave as it wants. For this Persona, there is an inability to comprehend why a written state-

**A bad day of fishing is still better than a good day of work!**

ment should prove sufficient to restrain a person's actions and behaviors. Since there is only a need for the bare minimum, not only will people with this Persona find the quickest and easiest route to acquire what they need, but they will also become lazy and inactive once a task is achieved. People with a Phlegmatic Persona are therefore not the most reliable or trustworthy employees since their "rules of thought" are based the tendency to work only for what is strictly necessary and not strive for better goals or proper conduct. A lack of drive to improve, advance, or expand are all typical characteristics for this Persona.

Though they may not admit it, Phlegmatic Personae are generally lazy and prefer to either spend the day procuring the necessary needs or resting comfortably on a bed or couch. For this Persona, a bad day of fishing is better than a good day at work. This Persona is characterized by a frequent need for personal space, and moments of complete inactivity. Sometimes even social interactions can seem invasive. Other times, the focus is on the family, especially the children. The Phlegmatic can be quite protective of its family members since it sees the family as an entity it owns. More people in the family provide a sense of protection.

Though there is a focus on providing basic needs  and protection for the family, emotions are not widely expressed. Phlegmatics will communicate love or care for another with practical objects or gifts, but rarely with true emotional empathy. However, even with the family, their underlying desire for stability will make them become anxious about change, including children's development and eventual separation from the family, as well as changes in routine.

## Gender Differences

Males with Phlegmatic Personae are generally attracted by material possessions and the accumulation of goods, whereas females with Phlegmatic Personae are interested in anything that can procure them an easy comfortable life that does not require effort.

Both males and females with Phlegmatic Personae are protective of their territory and their possessions. Xenophobia is a typical male trait of the Phlegmatic Persona, while compulsive, chronic laziness is more typical of female Phlegmatic Personae.

## Goals

The Phlegmatic Persona is programmed to conserve. It conserves energy outputs, possessions, and current states of being. It is therefore focused on the acquisition of material goods, and is not interested in improving a personal lifestyle, social status, or personal skills. A danger is seen and perceived strongly if money or possessions are taken away from a phlegmatic. There is a tendency to gravitate towards positions of care, like caring for their offspring, for animals, for the sick, for fauna and flora, towards the building industry, or towards industries of commercial exchange, like small grocery stores. Focus is generally on the most basic survival needs, and not on values like honesty, respect, and social rules.

## Effects on the Body

Phlegmatics possess a "phlegmatic" temperament stemming from an unbalanced function of the pancreas, which can cause digestive problems and hypoglycemic attacks (low level of sugar in the blood). This neural network can also interfere with balances in prolactin and insulin levels that can contribute to lethargy, panic, bipolar disorder, or abulia. Some will rely on food to appease their sense of emptiness but risk weight gain.

## Animal Analogy

The Phlegmatic Persona acts like a boar, a forager who survives with what is found. Their thick skin protects them from the natural elements, making them strong and resilient, but also willing to engage in hard confrontation when necessary. They are not particularly aggressive but are very defensive and territorial. Because of their kinesthetic tendencies, they will easily destroy fields with a lack of foresight while looking for their source of nourishment, and spend the rest of their time resting. As creatures of habit, boars will stay together as a small family group where all members of the clan contribute to the creation of a communal nesting sight. This nest doesn't move, is lined with vegetation, and is highly protected.

## Probable Reaction

The initial Phlegmatic reaction would be carelessness. If there is no drive for improvement, and this description cannot stimulate any practical use, then it is considered theoretical and as such discarded. First reactions are usually a lack of interest and understanding. When there finally is a desire for improvement, then each of the practical applications recommended in this book will have to be tried and tested. All reactions of a Phlegmatic Persona are direct and devoid of excessive premeditation.

# *REMINDER*

It is important to provide a concise reminder here that *the Persona you have identified as yours is not YOU*. Over time, you will have acquired the "virus-like" seed of a Persona that has begun to think for you, act for you, and even learn for you.

Its main purpose is to survive by lasting as long as possible within you, and by spreading itself onto others. If the Persona was made of your best intentions, it would be good to keep. Unfortunately, it is the result of long-term social conditioning and it is the cause of actual or potential sufferance from negative self-talk, doubt, individualism, bad decisions, and self-sabotage.

Your job now is to accept the challenge your life has presented to you and move forward. Remember that this is a self-challenge book. There are ways to overcome the Persona, to maintain a strong sense of integrity to your natural inner core, and to reach the peak of your performance abilities. The following chapters will help you begin your venture to a better and healthier life. Take action, challenge yourself, and rise above your past conditioning.

# Chapter 4
# When Coping
# Becomes Evading

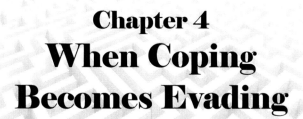

*"We don't see things
as they are, we see
things as we are."*
— The Talmud

Humans adapt to situations to survive. All human behavior is in fact a sum of adaptive mechanisms developed over time to ensure the survival of the species. We have an innate tendency to cope with difficult and physically challenging situations. The better we cope with weather, lack of food or water, infections, and physical or emotional pain, the longer and better we survive.

Both the subconscious and the conscious minds follow similar patterns of coping, with the greatest difference being fear. Rather than physical traumas, which is most feared by the subconscious, **a Persona's greatest fear is its inexistence.**

Whereas the subconscious mind will focus on problem-solving strategies to ensure the body's physical safety, the Persona often fixates on ineffective strategies that reconfirm its "rules of thought." Any attempt to criticize, deny, or dismantle the Persona is perceived as a threat to its life. For example, imagine a person that is suddenly dismissed from a job. The feeling of having lost career and prospects along with direction in life can be staggering for one's self-esteem. If this individual has developed a Nervous Persona in response to social conditioning and specific learned behaviors, it is likely that the Persona will react with resentment as a coping strategy.

Now that you have identified the Persona that resides in you while reading Chapter 3, there is one more preparatory phase before you face it and eradicate the power it may have over you.

*Understanding that the strategies your Persona uses to cope with mentally threatening events will help prepare you for the possible reactions you may*

*have while trying to step away from its power. At-*
*tempts to remove the Persona will be detected by it*
*and will instigate a specific evasive survival mecha-*
*nism to protect itself.*

Personae, like animals, tend to respond to threats to their survival in different ways. Some resort to fighting, some to escaping, some like to use camouflage, and others will simulate death or stand perfectly still so that predators will not notice them. Usually all protection methods are preceded by an alertness to threatening signals and a readiness to adopt their survival strategy. Signs like hair standing on end, aggressive behavior, immobility, or specific gestures communicate an animal's level of alertness. Your Persona will similarly identify your efforts to harm it and will engage its specific survival strategy. By noticing the signs of its survival strategy, you can learn to take control and overcome it. The evasive strategies of the Persona are rooted and powerful. Do not underestimate them.

## *Coping Strategies*

Regardless of the strategies used, personal evolution and life-threatening situations are the responsibility of the subconscious self and are not efficiently managed at the conscious level. However, the Persona likes to take control and use its own coping strategy to reconfirm its "rules of thought." With the following descriptions, you can analyze and identify patterns of self-defense mechanisms that may be activated by the Persona. The better you can recognize the Persona's patterns of behavior, the better you can regain control over it. This chapter is particularly dedicated to your preparation for the exercises of Chapter 5 in which you will be asked to recall past events and clear your mind. With these exercises, you may experience various reactions. Understanding how your Persona may respond to the exercises will help you be better prepared to achieve positive resolutions of past mental self-conditioning.

## *Typical Strategy for Sanguine Personae: Confusion*

Confusion is a prevailing defense mechanism that attempts to deny the overwhelming event. This typical strategy of Sanguine Personae includes 3 major approaches of denial:

1.  Completely deny the reality of the overwhelming event.

2.  Realize that something happened but deny its magnitude; minimize it.

3.  Perceive the problem and accept its intensity, but deny your responsibility for it.

Internal confusion and uncertainty is a strategy that purposefully rejects the real fact that one cannot go back in time to change the outcome of an overwhelming event. Confusion is caused by partial memory loss to reduce the pain associated with an event.

Frequently Sanguines will become insecure, and use memory repression as an attempt to avoid the direct confrontation with a sad, frustrating, or challenging event. The Sanguine Persona will make a person feel confused, without clear thoughts, and ensure attention is scattered and directed outward, avoiding self-reflection. With no introspection, the problem is overlooked in order to remain distracted.

For typical Sanguine Personae, survival is considered possible by obtaining recognition and confirmation from the social group, family members, as well as friends. Not only will this Persona try to cope through social support, but it will also encourage a person with this Persona to be more noticeable than others. A person with a Sanguine Persona will tap into social networks, politics, demagogy, mind games, sexual seduction, and social positions as a distraction from personal feelings.

*The Sanguine strategy is: the more visible you are, the more people you have who can help you.*

## *Typical Strategy for Lymphatic Personae:*
## *Apprehension*

Apprehensive acceptance of demanding, distressing, or frustrating situations is typical for the Lymphatic Persona. Anxiety, distress, concern, and hesitation are very common characteristics. A person with a Lymphatic Persona will be emotionally detached from the trauma and find distraction in low-energy activities to keep mentally active on other matters. Attention will wander, and many thoughts will appear at once.

Lymphatic Personae will want to take it slow, one thing at a time, defer, procrastinate, and remain in a state of detached observation. Limited response capabilities are generally accompanied by glandular hypo-functions in response to stress (such as low adrenaline and slow metabolism). By keeping everything in a state of constant observation and in slow motion, without jumping to a conclusion, a person with a Lymphatic Persona tries to avoid the responsibility of making choices and having to own the accountability of possible outcomes of these actions.

*The Lymphatic strategy is: the more you can procrastinate, the more time you can think, thus avoiding negative consequences of your actions.*

## *Typical Strategy for Nervous Personae:*
## *Resentment*

Nervous Personae generally crystallize into a state of resentment in which one enters because of an emotional hardening or "coming to terms with" a new condition. This rigid condition is accompanied by feelings of continuous struggle and hostility against the hard realities of life. Emotions are shut down and a stern, hard approach to life is embraced as a punishment to bear. Without being able to perceive suitable solutions to the problem, people with Nervous Personae become tense and emotionally shut-down, as though armor were built around them to show a strong façade or wall.

A person with a Nervous Persona will find refuge in an identity of power and control, relying on work and personal success to make them feel better. As the opposite of the "grouping" tendency, this Persona will create an emotional barrier and an "I can deal with it myself" attitude.

*The strategy is: individuality and emotionlessness will help maintain control.*

## *Typical Strategy for Melancholic Personae: Depression*

The Melancholic coping strategy is typically expressed as a condition of deep abandonment and depression. This Persona prompts feelings of persecution, oppression, and a lack of emotional energy. Feelings of purposelessness in life arise, which result in complete disengagement from regular routines. In an attempt to control the stress of the unsolved situation, escape from the external world takes place. The worse the situation seems, the more people with Melancholic Personae may curl into themselves in an introspective attitude, as though they were trying to disappear or escape from the realities of life. Some may try to invoke a higher power in search for help.

For most Melancholic Personae, the survival strategy is to have two sides to the self. The one remains unseen and secretive, while the other functions as an approachable interface which seeks attention and compassion from others. A person with a Melancholic Persona will seek seclusion and distance from situations of responsibility that may require them to step out of their depressed state, while still desiring sympathy from those around them. This Persona will also try to hide by blending in, acquiring a simulated identity or status, or by falling into an introspective depressive state.

*The Melancholic strategy is: if you seem weak, others will provide you with their energy and care.*

## *Typical Strategy for Bilious Personae:*
## *Frustration*

The coping strategy for the Bilious Persona is frustration and impactful reactivity with intense energy outputs of possible feelings of hate, annoyance, or complete changes in one's belief system (like no longer believing in a higher power). This strategy is accompanied by a general feeling of discontentment, bitterness, and an idea of living in an unjust world that provokes reactions of rage or reprisal.

A person with a Bilious Persona will tend to blame, attack, quarrel, or yell. Attention will be directed at a specific cause thought to be the source of the problem, and destructive behaviors will be addressed towards it. Survival is perceived possible only if one's actions are swift, impulsive, spontaneous, and aggressive because if you are emotionally expressive, you will appear strong and in control.

*The Bilious strategy is: if you want peace, prepare for war.*

## *Typical Strategy for Phlegmatic Personae:*
## *Immobilization*

Phlegmatic Personae typically express immobilization when seemingly overwhelming events take place, sometimes feeling numb or with low energy. This paralysis-like reactivity generates fatigue and neuromuscular inhibition.

A person with a Phlegmatic Persona will freeze into immobility and hold on to whatever they possess, whether it is their possessions, the people around them, or their convictions and traditions. They may also feel a sense of being frozen in time when trying to remember details surrounding a difficult event. They will physically try to touch objects in their vicinity or use food as emotional compensation to feel secure because their survival strategy is based on maintaining physical contact with the external world. They will often become emotionally inexpressive, assured that as long as they have their possessions, there is nothing they can or need to do.

*The Phlegmatic strategy is: the less you spend, the longer you survive; conserve.*

## *The Solution*

As you can see from the 6 coping strategies of the various Personae, none are effective because they fixate on a specific strategy without attempting to move on and beyond the problem. Even if the Persona in you doesn't match your usual coping strategy, it is important to keep in mind that there is only one effective coping strategy that can lead to overcoming dilemmas, challenges, and negative events: *Resolution.*

### Finding Resolution

People who achieve a coping strategy based on resolution find ways to create positive outcomes out of a negative event by becoming *proactive*. They actually do something about their new situation, develop a purposeful future orientation, and contribute positively to their society and environment as a result of their experience. Coined by the Austrian psychiatrist Viktor Frankl, the original term "proactive" did not refer to the action of being prepared for the future, as many people use it today, but suggested that one can find positive "meaning" in traumatic events. In his book, *Man's Search for Meaning*[11], Frankl explains that even under the worst circumstances, people can find meaning.

When you are truly proactive and find resolutions to your problems, you will experience adaptive and evolutionary changes. By making the most of the difficulties we encounter, we make the most of ourselves and can regain focus on a higher purpose in life. For the exercises of Chapter 5, the ultimate aim is to reach the resolution phase in which you become proactive about dismissing the Persona that resides in you, finding your best future orientation, and changing your stance.

However, if you ever feel like you are stuck in one of the Personae's coping strategies and have difficulty moving towards resolution, try to remember the typical reaction your Persona would have when threatened, and notice that the sabotage to overcome the challenge stems from it. The better you understand the Persona, the better you know how to be one step ahead of it. Be strategic! The Persona will systematically find ways to reconfirm its "rules of thought" and keep you stuck in a certain strategy. The only way to move beyond that strategy is to avoid corroborating the Persona's behavioral patterns. In other words:

## *Don't Use It! Lose It!*

At birth, the human brain contains approximately 100 billion neurons that are present but not interconnected. These neurons are formed during the first 16 weeks of gestation. Throughout life, the neural network is formed as information is input and connected to other neurons. These connections are called *dendrites* and are created with usage and repetition. Interconnections are shaped through nodes or intersecting dendrites. Information is thus transferred across a grid, producing the net architecture of our conscious mind. Nodes are intersecting points where the signal is amplified and re-transmitted. In our neural networks, these nodes would correspond to the intersection of the net of the conscious mind where information can be processed. Evolutionists think that it took us 350 million years to develop such a network capability and it is for this reason that we refer to the "glitch" being "evolutionary".

### Eliminating the Roadblocks

To illustrate this brain activity, imagine neurons are separate towns. To communicate between one town and another, roads are built. These roads are the dendrites or neural connections. If there is frequent travel between one town and another, the roads get more consolidated. The reverse is also true. Small towns can be completely ignored if unpaved dirt roads are not used. In our conscious mind, the center of an idea or thought would be like a city where many roads branch out.

As discussed in Chapter 3, the Persona germinates from the epicenter of an emotive shock of social rejection. Rather than making appropriate connections between thoughts, memories, and beliefs, the Persona creates detours on roads to other locations to ensure information passes by them. Therefore, it only accepts information that confirms its neural architecture and censures anything that contradicts its basic acquired database. Not only is the Persona formed by data that match its tendency and confirm its beliefs, but it also specifically selects, accepts, and stores events that are congruent to its model.

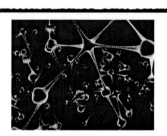

Neurons are cognitive units that become active only in relation to specific networks. Our neural networks are therefore the architecture of our conscious minds and our cognitive filters.

The Persona will create conditions in the real world that involve events that confirm its architectural rules. Anything that contradicts the model or does not confirm it is fought or ignored. Whereas normal learning separates new information into "I know this" or "I don't know this," with the main motive being "the more I know, the more I can survive;" the Persona will classify experiences as "this confirms" or "this doesn't confirm," with the main motive being "the more I can confirm, the deeper personal substantiation I can create." As neurons are activated, *mnestic traces* (memories) are stored. The patterns of neurons that activate simultaneously in response to an event will form associations which neuroscientists call *engrams*.

## Stop Feeding the Monster

The more the neural connections are used, the more ingrained they become. Just like the muscles in our body need regular exercise to grow strong or to stay in shape, our neural networks need to be constantly worked because neural connections can fade if they are not frequently used. For instance, a person might be born in Germany and have learned German in the first years of his life but, if he moves to America and does not continue to use German, the neural connections related to German will dissolve and he will lose the ability to speak German.

This is why a Persona will constantly need to "feed" itself with congruent information in the attempt to stay alive or grow stronger. The ancient wise people of India and China were perfectly aware of this when they tried to invent various methods of meditation to prevent the reinstallation of the Persona. Through meditation they were able to avoid the consequential routine that creates the state of validation of conscious conditioning. Our Persona instigates its corroboration by regularly finding or provoking episodes that confirm its basic thought process.

The next chapter proposes processes to remove, even if for a short moment, the biased structure of the Persona. Different activities, such as memory recall, can lead to the disconnection of dendritic structures. If these exercises are practiced properly, the failure to reconfirm the Persona's biased inputs can result in reactive responses, accompanied by anxiety, frustration, and unfamiliar feelings. Ultimately, "a system crash" or a strong sense of openness will indicate that the Persona has been hit and a clean network can be acquired.

This natural phenomenon can be used to your benefit, if you want to dissolve the unwanted habits and conditioning you have acquired. Because neural connections are formed through reinforcement and confirmation, the starting point of the remedy against the Persona is to avoid confirming its usual behaviors, habits, and beliefs.

However, it is important to remember that at the beginning, the Persona will feel threatened and will react with one of the coping strategies described earlier. Typical reactions include a sense of chaos, uncertainty, over-thinking, confusion, or instability, which confirm the Persona has been correctly identified. However, this state is also accompanied by an absence of forethought and it therefore allows a wider openness to signs in the surrounding environment without the biased lens of the Persona.

## Recalling What's Real

The memory recall techniques used in the next chapter are extremely simple but require a basic understanding of recollection mechanisms. When mentally searching for memories, we encounter a branched network of thoughts or recollections. A bit like performing an Internet search, a large ensemble of information regarding your query will appear. The more precise the search words in question, the more specific your answer will be. When thinking about "London," for example, you might think about England, the flag, the Queen, soccer hooligans, etc. This cluster of information is activated every time you think about a subject for which you have a previous database. Unknown words or symbols would not possess a database and therefore not provoke results for the search. Neural networks are associative entities that connect one experience to another with the criteria of similarity.

Our Persona uses a biased recalling strategy that associates only what confirms its neural architecture while deleting or omitting anything that contradicts its basic beliefs. For example, when recalling an episode where one of your actions caused problems for others, you might only recall a version of the facts that puts you on the side of being right. All memories acquired through a Persona are biased and revisited, corrected, and sometimes partially rebuilt, in the attempt to make them fit a model. For instance, a Persona will make you certain that you said something that in reality you never said. A Persona uses a biased database, a partial and subjective response system, and a filtered set of associations that we activate every time we perceive some stimulus from the external world.

Any information that we "know" already is classified in a fashion that is similar to the "bar code." A bar code attached to an object, once scanned, can provide a large amount of pre-installed information about the item. Once the information is stored in our memory, the simple scan stimulates its recognition and its label. When we see a real apple, a photo of an apple, a drawing of an apple, or hear the sound of the word "apple," we automatically resort to the label we carefully prepared for that object and associate it with the "fruit" category, the "food" category, etc.

Therefore, because of the mnestic trace or memory storage phenomenon, recalling does not only mean remembering an object or an event, it means recalling all the associations that we built along with that thought. A proper recalling technique can elicit a complete association of a neural network and uncover the seed of a Persona. It is for this reason that the next chapter begins with specific recall exercises before separation from the Persona can take place.

If you think you are devoid of any personal trouble, happy with yourself, and confident in what you do, allow yourself to reflect others to help them improve. If the people around you have difficulties and are ill, anxious, or depressed, they can cause disharmony in you as well. It is not possible to be truly happy amidst diseased and sad people, unless one lives in complete denial or detachment. Therefore, even when we feel good about ourselves, it is functional for us to understand and work on our conditions in order to help others and to create a balanced environment of coexistence.

*"The moment one definitely commits oneself, then providence moves too. All sorts of things occur to help one that would never otherwise have occurred. A whole stream of events issues from the decision, raising in one's favor all manner of unforeseen incidents and meetings and material assistance, which no man could have dreamed would have come his way."*

— *Goethe*

# Chapter 5
# Removing the Mask

*"Success depends upon previ-*
*ous preparation, and without*
*such preparation there is sure*
*to be failure."*
— *Confucius*

This chapter will hit the core of the self-challenge mental-ity. To break the power your Persona has over you, you are going to need your awareness and not your forethought. While your Persona lies strong, your deductive capabilities are too biased and cannot function as a reliable source of observation. You will need to put aside your preconceived notions, your as-sumptions, your suspicions, your superimpositions, and your analytical overlays. Your "what if?" attitude, your critical thinking, your doubts, and your negative self-talk will be of no use here. Your analytical abilities are best saved for the end of this chapter to find the hidden meanings these exercises have revealed to you.

*Analysis is like using a microscope; it's a great tool if you know what you are observing and if the lenses are clear. If your lenses are stained, you will continuously superimpose the blemish on everything you observe.*

The remedy you will find in this book is not aiming at tak-ing away your conscious awareness, but instead is aimed at clearing it from superimpositions. The removal of the condi-tions that bind us in subservience to a prejudiced perception of the world is a valued topic to ancient and medieval doctrines. Buddhism, Hinduism, and Taoism, for instance, were all sys-tems based on these exact premises. These systems aimed at the acquisition of a purely objective state of being, a very desir-able condition that, when applied on a large scale, can lead to the eradication of such phenomena as racism, social hatred and conflicts, family dysfunction, and emotional disease. One of the systematic methods of ancient times that was rediscovered dur-ing the middle ages was the system of *Alchemy*.

# *Alchemy Exercises*

The goal of Alchemy was to extract the quintessence from raw matter by removing impurities and crystallizing the life force extracted from the object. This process usually involved using an athanor (depicted here) or an alchemic oven.

In ancient times, Alchemy was used as a specialized approach to self-purification from acquired conditioning. Alchemy (from the Arabic *al-khymiyā'*, meaning the art of transformation) refers to spiritual and philosophic forms of investigation into the functions of nature by combining elements of chemistry, physics, medicine, metallurgy, and mysticism. Alchemists believed that everything is linked by one great force. Practiced for about 2,500 years throughout the world (Mesopotamia, Ancient Egypt, Persia, India, Japan, Korea, China, Ancient Greece, and Rome), this approach became a commitment to the attainment of knowledge in its purest form and through the physical transformation of the Alchemist's body. Since the time of the ancient Egyptians, a central point to their hermetic philosophy was the belief that the human body (the microcosm) was affected by the exterior world (the macrocosm) and that it was indispensable to purify one's existence and body to resonate with one's real, or "golden," nature. The general idea of philosophical alchemy was the purification of the individual through a sequential practice called Opus Magnum, or "the Great Oeuvre," which was composed of seven stages in three main phases:

1. **Nigredo** (rendering to black)

2. **Albedo** (purification to white)

3. **Rubedo** (activity in red)

Adhering to the order of these phases with the suggested exercises will provide you the ability to experience a temporary but insightful unbiased state of mind. Some may find the motivation of a positive social group or a coach who is familiar with this technique helpful. The more the removal of the Persona is pursued, and the more constant you are with your practice, the more you can clean the lens of your vision. However, sometimes just a glimpse of an experience is all it takes to understand where a path can lead.

## Nigredo (Blackness)

According to the beliefs of Alchemists, a decaying process is essential in order to reduce impurities down to a single problem. Everything that had an origin eventually expires, passing through decomposition and transmutation, into a new state of being. This means that even unpleasant and difficult periods of your past had and have a place in your life. Psychologically, this refers to the need to overcome one's defects through the unification and transformation of all defective activities of your brain.

Flaws can be conquered if unified in a congruent ensemble, because they stem from the same source. In this case, the flaw refers to the Persona you have identified as the seed that germinates in you. Our organism does the same with bacteria and foreign elements. When bacteria are identified, they are destructured and dissolved, and the waste is expelled or separated from the body.

Once the Persona has come into contact with fears, pain, chaos, death, and other dark states, it can eventually seek a way to work through these and begin a purification process. When the "bad" or impure parts of our mental conscious functions are identified and isolated into a uniform black mass, it is possible to see their structure and origin. Neural superimpositions must be removed in order to see with clarity and function with a clean mind.

Because the state of Nigredo is associated with a higher production of melatonin, a hormone released during sleep or in the presence of darkness as well as in states of reminiscence of past negative events, be prepared for a period of mood fluctuations, introversion, a slightly reduced libido, and deep self-reflection when you are going through this phase. These effects are brief but the outcomes of the exercises can be stimulating and life-changing.

The three stages of the Nigredo phase are:

1. **Calcination**: Issues are raised. The Persona is identified (the black mass).

2. **Dissolution:** Issues are dissolved into specific past experiences. One identifies where and when conditioning was accepted.

3. **Separation:** Issues are divided into distinct chains of recollections and a first transition occurs.

## Calcination

### Exercise 1

This exercise is aimed at the root of your Persona. As discussed in Chapter 3, the "virus-like" seed of your Persona was planted by moments of intense or traumatic rejection, which initiated your state of Anomie. The more rejection you encountered and the more you reconfirmed the "rules of thought" of your Persona, the more fertilizer you placed on the seed to allow it to grow into the weed you now have. To recultivate your mental garden, begin by attacking the weeds and shedding light on why they invaded your garden in the first place.

For this exercise, you will have to recall 10 episodes of rejection. Search for the most significant ones, episodes that really contributed to a sharp or sudden change in your life. Childhood and teenage experiences are the most common epicenters, but also recall the ones that most adults try to forget. Take your time; this is the most important exercise. The more recollections you have, the more a pattern will begin to emerge. Try to understand the underlying pattern of rejection you have experienced and begin to understand how these episodes have affected your thought patterns.

While doing this exercise, try to be as precise as possible. It is important that you hand-write the descriptions of the episodes rather than type them, so that your muscles are engaged while you remember the events. Allow the words on the pages to flow through your pen and write everything as it comes to your mind.

Without thinking about order, structure, grammar, or clarity, focus on the particulars of the recollections and allow yourself to recover your forgotten memories. Describe the time and day of the event, who was there, where it took place, the clothes people were wearing, what was being said, the moments that preceded and followed the event, the emotions you felt, etc. If you do not provide the exact moments, your mind is providing a label for the memory and allowing the emotions to remain boxed in. Recalling with precision and detail allows the associated emotions to surface.

If, after 10 recollections, you have not yet felt profound emotions emerge from the depths of your memories or have not discovered an underlying pattern of events, start again and search for the life-altering rejection you endured. The stronger your Persona is, the more it tries to hide its roots from you. Keep digging while bearing in mind that strong rejections will not be easy to remember because your Persona will attempt to sabotage this process and encourage you to abandon it. When you recall rejection, one of the most probable reactions will be to feel rejection. You might start becoming critical about the book, the author, and the process, or you might begin doubting yourself, procrastinating, and avoiding the efforts. However if you stop here, you stop your progress. Be prepared to manage rejection for the effort will be worthwhile.

### Dissolution

The stage of Dissolution can be accomplished by the recollection of specific events pertaining to your Persona. Every Persona has a "core" made of a specific critical phase associated with rejection. If a chain of episodes that are the expression of that core is remembered, an entire neural network is reactivated simultaneously and becomes ready to be reworked.

To use a term in artificial intelligence research, we will call these episodes "cognitrons." A cognitron is a chain of perceptions and memories that can be activated. For instance, "anger" will activate all the ideas, perceptions, and memories related to anger. This exercise can be worked alone or more preferably with the help of a coach or a friend that is following the same process and knows about this technique.

*Exercise 2*

Recall at least 10 episodes of specific actions as per your Persona indicated in the following table. For instance, if you have a Sanguine Persona, recall episodes where you made other people feel undervalued.

Begin by taking a blank page and writing today's date. Recall a first episode that comes to mind according to your Persona. Try to remember the date of when that episode took place as well as all the details related to that episode (what preceded it, what were its outcomes, who or what was involved, where did it take place, what was said, how was it said, what was the body language, etc.), just like you did in the previous exercise. Be specific. The more details you can provide, the more your patterns of behavior will become obvious. Allow the thoughts to flow through the movements of your hand as you write.

Once you have completed this exercise, take a look at the episodes you have recalled and see if you can find a pattern of

| *PERSONA* | *EPISODES TO REMEMBER* |
|-----------|------------------------|
| *Sanguine* | Episodes when you undervalued other people |
| *Lymphatic* | Episodes when you limited yourself by hesitating or over thinking |
| *Nervous* | Episodes when you hid something from others |
| *Melancholic* | Episodes when you abandoned something or someone in a time of need |
| *Bilious* | Episodes when you blamed someone or something else for your mistakes |
| *Phlegmatic* | Episodes when you put up with unwanted situations |

behavior. Did someone or something impose a belief pattern on you? Do you remember seeing similar behaviors in people who you may have looked up to during your developmental years? Is it possible that your actions are imitations of others and not your own invention? Generally, an "aha!" moment surfaces and the "rules of thought" of the Persona within you become apparent. If not, perhaps you should dig a little deeper and be more honest and sincere with yourself.

The ancient Alchemist saying, "*When the darkened matter is polished, it can also reflect light better than other colors,*" was used to mean that you can see the patterns in your past actions even if they were wrong. This insight should allow you to see your actions more objectively and propel you towards separation from the moments in your life that are holding you back.

*You should realize that these actions are outcomes of your Persona and are not characteristic of you as a person.* With the rest of the exercises, you will increasingly come to understand how your Persona has caused most of the difficult moments in your life and how to change the route of your future course.

## Separation

In this stage, you will recall moments of doubt. Doubts are moments of hesitation and uncertainty because of a lack of trust. Whether you do not trust yourself, others, or some information presented to you, disbelief and suspicion arise, causing a mental blockage on how to proceed. As the opposite of certainty, doubt is the questioning process of the conscious mind that overpowers subconscious intuition. A questioning mind is good, but it is limiting when biased. To learn to trust your subconscious abilities, you must first understand the patterns of mental processing that block you.

Doubt can cause one to refrain from taking action or responsibility in a situation that requires certainty and confidence. Try to recall episodes of doubt that resulted into some significant effect. A lost opportunity, a social situation that was unclear and created discomfort, a choice that you had to make and you refrained from making, a situation that required your firm decision based on a certainty but you could not perform, etc.

*Exercise 3*

Using several sheets of paper, recall 5 conditions of unresolved issues of doubt in your life. If you are still bothered by the times you doubted about something significant, it's worth remembering those events for this exercise. If you are currently indecisive about this exercise, unsure about which episodes to recall, then you doubt right now and you can use this moment in time as your first episode.

On the first sheet of paper, write "Episode #1" at the top and begin describing everything you remember with as much detail as you can. Do not think about the sentences, the grammar, or punctuation. Allow your pen to flow freely. Only when you are finished with this episode should you move on to number two. Be very specific and go back as many times as needed to recall who was in the episode, what happened exactly, when it happened, what time of day it was, how you got into the situation, where it took place, and any other detail that you think is relevant.

This exercise is very important because doubt is like a knot in a garden hose. The most critical "knots" in our neural networks are reactively created after un-decisive and uncertain moments. These knots block the natural electrical current in our neural connections and stop our flow of ideas. If we were to consider the mind like a computer, unresolved issues that cause uncertainty are the programs that run in the background. Like in a computer that has too many processes active at the same time, unresolved moments of doubt will slow down your intuition and your induction abilities. The more files you have open, the more energy is being spent trying to make sense of these issues, and the less energy there is to concentrate on the more important issues of your life. Uncertainty stops you from moving forward because it takes so much of your attention to run in circles around it. To close the files, think about the issues of doubt that are still bothering you.

*Exercise 4*

This is the last stage of the Nigredo phase and it consists of separating various elements from the cognitrons found. This phase is best addressed with a simple free association exercise.

Returning to the written memories of Exercises 2 and 3,

pick a subject, a person, or a concept that you wrote down. You will instinctively know which word you should use, so it is best to follow your gut feelings on which words you want to select for this exercise. Write the first word you chose at the top of a new page. Before you go further, free your mind and get ready to undergo a fast-paced procedure.

When you're ready to begin, say the word or name out loud and write the first related word that comes to your mind. Be as quick as possible. It may even be in your best interest to allow someone else to write the words down for you. The more time it takes for you to come up with a free association, the higher the chance is that you are not associating but rather thinking logically about it.

Continue to write down all the words that strike you until no more associations come to mind, without stopping to question the logic behind your associations. If emotions arise, write these down beside the words that evoked them.

When you have finished with the first word association, pick another word or subject from Exercise 2 or 3 and repeat the process. This exercise should be applied at least 10 times and may take a few days to complete. If strong emotions are evoked that stop you from continuing the exercise, allow them to come to the surface and take note of their manifestation. Continue only when you feel ready to continue.

By the end of the four Nigredo exercises, you will discover a surge of novel feelings and a fresh sense of motivation. This is the sign that you are on the right track. It will feel like you are seeing the world with a new set of eyes, marveling at the sights and experiences you would have otherwise considered common. The smallest things will give you a rush of awe and wonder. You will feel enlightened.

If you still have feelings of doubt, confusion, or frustration, your Nigredo phase is incomplete. Do some more exercises to free yourself from your Persona. Return to the Calcination stage and review your work, see if you needed to be more honest in your recollections, or reveal something your mind has been hiding from you. Move on to Dissolution and Separation in the same way and be reassured that this process takes time, dedication, and determination. The strength of your will is being tested against the strength of your Persona and only you can decide which will win.

By bringing your awareness to where you are mentally blocked, you begin to understand where you are blocked in life, and vice versa. The more detail you can provide in the exercises, the more you can clear the "knots" in your mind created by your Persona and the more you can understand the circumstances under which you created and continue to create doubt in your life. This process will help bring clarity and help you complete the subsequent exercises.

## *Albedo (Whiteness)*

If you have done the previous exercises properly, your actual state is now slightly different. You start feeling lighter and you might have some burst of intense clarity and happiness. *Albedo* literally means the measure of how much light is reflected by a surface; Albedo refers to the period after the darkest state is conquered. In Albedo, your organism starts to set itself free from the previous limitations of the Persona and starts to slowly appear through your reflective actions. In this phase, you will find yourself reflecting others and you will see that what happens around you is a result of your internal state.

To better understand how the world around you is a reflection of who you are, you will first need to reflect the environment and work almost like a mirror to events and behaviors. In Alchemy, this phase includes the processes of "conjunction" with external events, "fermentation," or release of energy, and "distillation," or unobstructed interaction with external events.

This state corresponds to what the ancient Yogis used to call "absorption" or meditation. Because you're like a sponge at this stage, highly sensitive to external influences, it is important to be aware that your environment can impact your direction and purpose without you realizing it. You must therefore be selective of the surroundings you choose while being in Albedo. Try to find an environment that promotes health and clarity. Furthermore, this state is accompanied by a release of serotonin, a neurotransmitter that induces a state of coherent philosophical behavior and general well-being.

## The Bulb Analogy

As an analogy for Albedo, consider a light bulb. The bulb is the structure that allows energetic emissions and light to shine. If you cover the bulb with your personal design, those images will be cast off on to the surfaces throughout the room or the bulb may emit a very dull light.

During the Nigredo phase, you may have noticed that bulb was covered with colors, pictures, fixed icons, and dark smudges. The more that covers the bulb, the feebler the emitted light becomes and the more shadows are cast on the surrounding surfaces. If the light bulb is cleaned, the light can shine freely again. The Albedo phase will allow you to remove the coatings created by the Persona and see the world with a clear unbiased light. Your clarity will also shine brightly onto others, allowing them to gain inspiration from you.

In line with the light bulb analogy, the neural networks of our brains are the physical parts of the bulb including the element, the glass, and the metal structure. Similarly, our consciousness is the equivalent to the radiance or light cast off by the bulb. With the help of the Albedo phase, we can shed pure light and might prompt illumination that allows us to "see" the world without filters and superimpositions, and help others better understand or "see" their own problems or conditions.

The three stages of the Albedo phase are:

1. **Conjunction:** The coming together of the internal state and external events, providing a deeper understanding of the reflective behavior of the mind in contrast with the self-centered one.

2. **Fermentation:** The reaction given by following external events and seeing in them the reflection of one's internal state, which results in more energy.

3. **Distillation:** By contemplating the past and engaging the present, informed choices about the future become clear.

## Conjunction

*Exercise 5*

The state of conjunction is characterized by the realization that the events around you mirror you and that you mirror your environment. For this exercise, you will need to have a notebook with you at all times, in which you can write down the events that happen to you. You will soon notice that what "happens" around you is a reflection of very quick thought processes that you had running through your mind. You may, for example, notice a door slam loudly only a few milliseconds after you had thoughts about closing a liaison with someone. As another example, you may be given a gift out of the blue that is the same item you wanted to buy for yourself the next day. You may also have a difficult question in mind only to see the answer appear as an image on a poster.

Now that you have reduced the background noise produced by the incessant self-talk of the Persona with the Nigredo exercises, you are ready to hear what life has to say. Carry this notebook and write down your observations about the events that happen around you.

The amount of time dedicated to this exercise depends on the occurrences in your life and your personal determination. You may be able to read signs, identify patterns, and discover a future orientation in a few weeks or a few months. You may even choose to continue writing in your notebook throughout the years to come, always being open to the events around you.

> *Life whispers its magic quality to you all the time, but only when you are fully open to hearing the messages can you benefit from its guidance.*

## Fermentation

This stage corresponds to the activity of being conjoined to the perception of the external world. For instance, you could be sitting in a park, on a beach, or in an open field doing nothing but noticing what happens in your mind after you hear a sound or see an event take place. Try to take note of your senses. What are your reactions to the things you see, smell, hear, or feel?

*Exercise 6*

Using the same notebook from the exercise of the Conjuction stage, write what it is you are noticing and the associations you make with external stimuli. Go to a location where you can sit and objectively observe the environment around you, writing down what you notice in a few words. Below these words, in brackets, write the feelings (happy, sad, angry) or sensations (hungry, cold, pain) provoked by your observations.

To learn how to perceive, you must see things for what they are, not how your mind filters them, so allow yourself several 30-60 minute sessions over a few weeks. By concentrating on what happens outside of you and noticing the reactions within you, you begin to develop synchronicity with life's events.

## Distillation

*Exercise 7*

For the stage of perception distillation, you should be in a quiet place to perform the exercise so you can listen to what happens inside your internal senses. Take a sheet of paper and divide it into two columns. At the top of the left column, write "Sensories." At the top of the right column, write "Constructs." When you are ready to begin, take note of anything that comes to your mind and write <u>everything</u> down.

If it is a feeling (happy, sad, angry), a sense (hungry, cold, pain), a taste (bitter, sweet, warm), a color (silver, red, dark), a smell (foul, sharp, floral), or a noise (whoosh, bang, creek), write it in the left column under "Sensories." If it is an object you can label (horse, helicopter, Egypt, philosophy, Asian), write it in the right column under "Constructs."

To differentiate between the real signs life has to offer and the signs you want to see, you must learn to distinguish between real perceptions and the mental noise caused by personal associations with a perception. Take the time to do this exercise several times over a few weeks. The aim of this exercise is to use your objective perception.

An enhanced yet unbiased perception of the environment is not only a very important tool for self-development, but it can also allow you to better interact with the events you encounter. For example, if you're driving a car and you have a better and broader perception of your surroundings, you'll notice things that would have otherwise passed below the threshold of your cognition and prevent accidents better than before.

The exercises of this chapter have been extracted by practices developed at Stanford Research Institute in the 1970s, while testing Extra Sensorial Perceptions, and were used to find the proper distinctions between real perceptions and personal constructs of the conscious mind. They make major differences in the way we can perceive the world around us and are worth the time and effort in doing them. In fact, the better they are achieved, the more you can clean the lens of your vision by freeing yourself from the power of your Persona.

All of the exercises in the Nigredo and Albedo phases are not only very powerful, but since they were developed under laboratory conditions, if practiced extensively, they will allow your mind to expand to a level of clarity that no other present technique can provide. Your heightened awareness and shrewd perception will enable you to intuitively and swiftly adapt your movements and direction in order to achieve clarity.

## Rubedo

An increase in warmth and light from cellular activity was seen by Alchemic traditions as the "reddening" process, or the complete release of heat and energy. At this phase, all cells will produce more energy in the infrared range and therefore produce a coherent heat that will disperse in the environment.

At the Albedo phase, great insights are possible and bursts of wisdom and well-being might be experienced, but only in the Rubedo phase is one's purification complete. Disease, for instance, becomes impossible in this phase. Once the Rubedo phase is complete, energy, internal power, and coherence become strong enough to impact the physical and social environments without being negatively affected.

The Albedo state of "reflectiveness" is considered an intermediate state and must "come alive" with "blood" or the "redness of life." The warmth and energy obtained in Albedo need to be released back in the world with Rubedo. This is similar to tribal adolescent rites of passage, which will be described in Chapter 6, which include a final stage in which the discoveries made through introspection are brought back to the clan with the aim of serving a greater good.

When your conscious and subconscious minds are completely integrated, you can embrace the best of your human capacities. Rubedo corresponds to the release of dopamine, an important neurotransmitter involved in cognition, creativity, motivation, and reward. The high release of this neurotransmitter can sometimes be perceived as a state of full awakening in the present world, with programmatic and pro-active attitudes, clear decision-making capabilities, and constructive determination.

The only stage of the Rubedo phase is:

1. **Coagulation**: Fresh insights and knowledge can be incorporated into the world and will inspire positive changes in individuals and groups of people. At this stage, an accelerated rate of synchronicity between the external world and the body is achieved, as well as a sense of suspension and timelessness. Specific brainwaves are generated which contribute to a state in which you continuously feel united with your external surroundings. The sympathetic (or stimulant) nervous system, and the parasympathetic (or relaxing) nervous system are activated at the same time, even if for a very short time, in bursts. These two opposing systems are usually activated at different times and in very different conditions. However, in this last stage, you are relaxed and alert simultaneously, thus able to make the most of the signs you receive, and always ready for action.

The next chapter will explain how you can find the future orientation that best suits you at the cellular level. You were born with certain talents and abilities and when you learn to be synchronous with your inner self, your can reach your real potential and hit the targets you set for yourself.

But before you begin to search for your future orientation and your life goal, make sure that the Persona in you has been completely destructured. *Do not try to rush.* Though most readers will want to read through the book without actually going through the exercises, or just merely thinking about them, all the stages in this chapter need to be completed in full or there will be a tendency to fall back into previous habits. You might read through this material for personal knowledge only, but many of the concepts will not make as much sense as they do after you experiment with a different state of perception.

It might take you between a few weeks and a few months to go through the exercises. Some may even choose to follow the exercises as part of a lifestyle change, always being synchronous with their environment, open to the signs and events around them, and always being aware of the ability a Persona can have to regerminate when least expected.

No improvements in life can be achieved unless the initial efforts are made. Step away from the "rules of thought" you previously used and break away from the attitudes that reconfirm the Persona. You have been conditioned for many years, and you will need some time to de-condition yourself now. The Persona gets reestablished through habits and routines, so you must occasionally find unusual places to escape from the routines of your daily environment where you can take the time to destructure the Persona. Feel free to change your location whenever you sense the Persona is germinating in you, and run through the exercises of this chapter again.

If you are having trouble being motivated and determined, find support in others who have either already worked their way through the book or are willing to do it with you, while making sure the "rules of thought" of the Persona are not brought into play. Energy is increased when you have positive encouragement.

*"The most successful men in the end are those whose success is the result of steady accretion. . . It is the man who carefully advances step by step, with his mind becoming wider and wider, and progressively better able to grasp any theme or situation, persevering in what he knows to be practical, and concentrating his thought upon it, who is bound to succeed in the greatest degree."*

*— Alexander Graham Bell*

# Chapter 6
# Your Inner
# Compass

*"Challenging the meaning of life is the truest expression of the state of being human."*
— *Victor Frankl*

After doing the exercises of Chapter 5, you should feel more in tune with the environment around you and have an innate sense of what is right for you. By means of a constant awareness of the different Personae that can germinate in you and in others, you should now have the ability to understand and respond appropriately to blockages or doubts Personae can create in your achievements. You should also be able to separate yourself from the power a Persona can have and be connected to your environment with your fresh ability to use your natural intuition. These skills are the foundation you need to adhere to your inner core, be synchronous with your body, and find the positive future orientations best suited for you. These are the initial steps required before this chapter can help you be in touch with your inner core, in order to reach your greatest potential, using your innate talents and abilities.

### *Who you are is the sum of the qualities that distinguish you from all others.*

In ancient Rome, the "Talent" was a unit of measurement for both weight and money, similar to the British pound (£). The term comes from the Latin *telentum* and from the Ancient Greek *talanton* meaning "a scale." It referred to a talent-weight of precious metals like gold and silver, and was therefore used as a measure of value. Nowadays we use the word "talent" to indicate a natural predisposition to perform an action better than others. The value of a person is measured by the actions he or she can perform towards the related environment. Increases in value are determined by the quality, need, and uniqueness of those talents.

### The Gene-Environment Interaction

You are essentially a unique combination of a physical entity, a conscious processor, a subconscious awareness, and a sum of external forces that synchronize you with the outer world in order to act as a carrier of a specific function of interaction with your surroundings. All of these parts work cohesively to form the life you are living. Changes in one part elicit changes in another.

The body is made of 100 trillion cells. Every cell is connected to every other cell in the body. Cells have their individual life and purpose but also function as a coordinated whole. When cells stop working in harmony with one another, diseases arise and the organism weakens. In addition to a physical body, we are endowed with a brain function that greatly contributes to our perception of reality. The overall activity of the brain's cortex results in what we call our consciousness, and often what we define as our truths. Along side is the subconscious, a unifying intelligence that guides our cells at every millisecond of our lives below our cognitive threshold (it works even if we are not aware of it). All processes that take place at a higher speed and below our perception pertain to the domain of our subconscious mind.

As organisms, we live immersed in a medium with which we continuously interact. The air we breathe, the sounds we hear, the electricity in the atmosphere, the warmth of the sun, and the communication signals we receive from others are all examples of external conditions that directly and indirectly affect our life, development, and adaptations. It is important to realize that, *for the sake of personal evolution as human beings, we are not, and will never be, independent from our environment.* The modern imposed model that suggests we seek independence is false and dangerous. Complete independence is naturally impossible. While Chapter 1 explains that our attitude and consequent activities contribute to our surrounding conditions, the reverse is also true in that our surrounding conditions also influence us. The environment shapes our physical state, our personal intentions, and our directions in life. The environment has such an impact that we can assume that *the state of your nearest environment is a reflection of yourself.*

The way you react to your environment determines your *Phenotype.* As mentioned in Chapter 1, your Phenotype is the combination of your genetic makeup and your adaptation to your environment. You are who you are because of your relationship with your social environment. This is your current stance. If you are unhappy with your present condition, there are two possible causes:

1. You have a wrong attitude in regards to your environment.

2. You are in an environment that is wrong for you.

## Start with the Heart

Positive integration with others, with a positive attitude, is vital since it allows you to expand your goals. Self-help approaches have a tendency to instigate a sense of "only you:" a focus on your well-being and self-discovery without consideration for others.  But it is in the non-individualistic, interdependent goals that you can find stronger motivation and will.

The search for the greater good inspired wise people of the past to look for a personal standard that allowed mutual acceptance, cooperation, and productivity. As Confucius once said,

> *"To put the world right in order, we must first put the nation in order; to put the nation in order, we must first put the family in order; to put the family in order, we must first cultivate our personal life; we must first set our hearts right."*

Starting with the heart, we must remember that at the heart of our self, stands the core of our attitudes, and from there our value is born. Many great people have understood that being a person of value is more significant than being a person of success and, in doing so, they have directly recognized the importance of integrity.

Confucius, who lived from 552 to 479 BC, is the most influential Chinese philosopher and educator in history. Among his most important teachings was the concept of *Ren Jen*. It is the sum of all human virtues, and considered a quality every person should strive to achieve.

The teachings of Confucius were quite practical and entirely based on common sense, natural bearings, moral attitude, empathy, and mutual understanding. Moral attitudes refer to the currency of good exchange or cooperation with others as a code of social interaction. There would be no morality without social interface. Your attitude is your bearing in life and is completely under your control. To quote Viktor Frankl, the inventor of Logotherapy,

> *"Everything can be taken from a man but one thing: the last of the human freedoms — to choose one's attitude in any given set of circumstances, to choose one's own way."*[12]

Among Confucius' wisdom were 5 main ethical attitudes that emerge when we live in harmony within our natural social "whole" and are observed phenomena of healthy social relationships. To better internalize these 5 Internal Attitudes, take a look at your left hand. The left side of the body is connected to the right hemisphere of the brain, which is responsible for most of your symbolic processes and your self-image. Count from the pinky towards the thumb; in doing so, you are indirectly triggering the right hemisphere of the brain to remember these attitudes.

## *5* Internal Attitudes

1. **Wisdom:** The capacity to produce understanding and good judgment after evidence.

2. **Integrity:** The adherence to moral attitudes, beliefs, and principles with commitment and dedication to something or someone, producing a reliable, strong, and trustworthy character.

3. **Sincerity:** The honorable and honest attitude that draws respect and admiration from others.

4. **Empathy:** The gentle, compassionate, and benevolent consideration and care for others.

5. **Respect:** The attitude of modest demureness and good mannerism that allows the adhesion to and acceptance of a mutually considerate behavior.

If you have trouble remembering these 5 Internal Attitudes, remember what you will become if you practice them:

### *W.I.S.E.R.*

We can only accept these attitudes if they truly work as an inspiration for our behavior and if they serve the cause of living in unity with others. Do not accept them just because they are presented to you. You must try them out and exercise them with the awareness of their effect. If you are still bearing in mind the analogy of the bow and arrow explained in Chapter 1, consider this job as preparing your bow. Once you have understood and embraced these 5 Internal Attitudes, you can start building your bow, beginning with the very core.

### Ideas on How to Be W.I.S.E.R.

To exercise Wisdom, the next time you debate with someone, try to understand his or her point of view instead of your own. Don't place judgment on the concept the person is expressing, but understand why he or she is expressing it.

To apply Integrity, stick to the promises and agreements you have made. If you commit mistakes, be upfront, accept responsibility, and make up for it.

Sincerity can be trained by saying what you truly think, in all cases, without reservation. Though this attitude carries the risk of exposing yourself completely, it also provides an extremely clear environment where friendship, love, and leadership can thrive.

Empathy is the capacity to resonate with other people's emotions. To feel what others feel, you must have a near-"telepathic" sympathy for them. Observe their emotional state and mirror it so that you can better understand it.

To implement Respect, try to be considerate of others' ways of expressing ideas and feelings, and be sensitive to their time, work, views, and desires. During a conversation, you might not agree with their perspective but still respect their opinion. Forms of respect include genuine greetings and salutations, ceremonies and rituals, decorum, and politeness.

These attitudes, when really understood and practiced together, will keep you away from antipathies and self-destructive behaviors that obscure the perception of your inner character. Additionally, performing the following 5 External Attitudes will more easily reveal your inner character, which has the potential to direct you. To reach your core, you must remove the shell.

## *5 External Attitudes*

When you interact with your surroundings, either social or biological, exercise these 5 External Attitudes and observe how they impact your life. To internalize these attitudes, look at your right hand and count from the thumb towards the pinky. The right side of your body is connected to the left hemisphere of your brain, which is in charge of logical processing and organized methods or actions. Your left hemisphere needs to know what to expect in order to perceive it. To help you further remember these 5 External Attitudes, take note of the fact that in order to be fully aware of the signs around you, you must be **R.E.A.D.Y.**

1. **Reject Rejection:** The fear of negative outcomes is limiting. Reject it and be true to yourself.

2. **Expect Signs:** Stay alert and attentive to events and signs as indicators of your optimal path in life.

3. **Accept the Signs:** Trust your subconscious mind's ability to interpret meaning behind happenings.

4. **Detect the Pattern:** Understand the pattern of your signs and learn from your achievements and mistakes.

5. **Yield:** Let go. Let events propel you as though you were "surfing the waves."

## 1. Reject Rejection

Love and a sense of belonging are the foundations of motivation. A sense of belonging is often required to form a social group but this frequently leads to a standardized social assembly. The sheep thus follow the shepherd without objection. Individualism, on the contrary, starts when you begin to think for yourself, sometimes stepping far away from the herd. Unfortunately, stepping away from the mass can also result in a sense of depression and hostility. For some people, being unique is a challenge that is embraced in becoming individualistic and detached, but we should remember that doing the opposite of what the masses do is not always an original move. Sometimes this reaction is even harnessed with reverse psychology by occult sellers. In the case of substance abuse, detaching yourself from the social group is cowardly and irresponsible, and also makes you much less than unique in that you have fallen into the hands of a new social group with none of the attitudes mentioned earlier.

What is right for an individual is not always what is largely accepted in society but it is often by having the strength of being an outsider that we can probe our inner principles and be true to ourselves. To be true to yourself is higher in value than blindly following fashions or fads. Once you find your inner value, you will be able to share it with the collective; you will have gained knowledge and deeper perceptions. The right alternative to following the masses, being blinded by the collective, or seeking individuality by moving away from one group and into another, is to *behave "for" the collective.*

In some cultures, this phase is represented as a rite of passage where the adolescent leaves the group in search of his qualities and comes back with something to offer. It is a form of introspection with the aim of serving a greater good. According to the French Ethnographist and Folklorist Arnold Van Gennep[13], rites of passage have three stages:

1. Separation

2. Liminality

3. Incorporation

During the first stage, the person withdraws from the social group and begins his personal path, thus moving away from the previous "clan" rules. The second stage is constituted by the time spent rebalancing. The detachment from the social environment leads to a personal reorientation (self-discovery) and directs the way towards the third stage. In the third stage, the person re-enters the social clan, having completed the task and conquered the difficulties of individualization. Notice that this is similar to the Alchemic 3-part model seen in Chapter 5.

Understanding that one of the main reasons why people continue to follow the herd is the fear of rejection from the social group is a very important first step in becoming aware of your inner core. *By rejecting the fear of rejection, you can begin to allow your instincts, emotions, and inner thoughts to guide you.* By rejecting the fear of failure, you can start to operate more freely in your environment.

Rejection is the lead actor in the common adolescent's theatrical production. It is seen in many forms and it demonstrates a natural evolutionary tendency to create character. The fact that age progresses you to an adult does not mean you have conquered the challenges of this adolescent phase. In fact, several unhealthy behaviors in adults are a result of failed "initiatory" phases.

During adolescence, the neural network rewires and branches away from the teachings of the clan or family. Rejection is therefore the necessary drive that allows individualization. Unfortunately for most adolescents, turning to cliques and other social groups in search of a new niche of acceptance becomes the next trap unless the liminality stage is completed enough to persevere in the value of individuation and properly adhere to the 5 Internal Attitudes.

When trying to maintain balance and harmony in adherence to your inner core, it is imperative to be careful with the use of rejection. If there is too much rejection from others or the rejection is too strong, it causes self-doubt. In addition, rejecting others can bring forth paranoia, suspicion, skepticism, and mistrust. Rejection can be a dangerous enemy of self-respect and personal strength and it often undermines the energy output of individuals. It is therefore important to reject at the right time and in the right amount, and to also understand the purpose and meaning behind rejection.

Rejection offers information on the person who is performing the action and not on the object of rejection. If a person is rejecting another, the problem is owned and expressed by the rejecter. Rejection communicates the rejecter's perception of others, filtered by personal memories, belief systems, priorities, idiosyncrasies, and preconceptions. It precisely mirrors the actual opinion of the external world of the rejecter and the events and circumstances he is experiencing.

When others reject you, do not commit the mistake of using this as a criterion of judgment for yourself. No information on you is gathered through rejection, only information on the rejecter. If you offer something and it is not approved or harshly rejected, this only means it is not appropriate for the social environment where you offered it; it does not mean that what you have to offer is universally invalid.

For example, when Nikola Tesla, one of the greatest inventors of all times, proposed his alternated current (AC) system to Thomas Edison, he was harshly criticized, ridiculed, and accused of causing harm to creatures who could be electrocuted by his invention. Edison's rejection of Tesla's invention was not a reflection of the system itself, since AC was a perfect concept, but it was a reflection of Edison's moral and intellectual faults. That same offer that is rejected in certain environments will be well accepted and praised under different circumstances. AC currents are now widely used and provide our main source of electrical energy. It is for this reason that evaluating your stance requires you to assess your environment and the ratio between your sense of belonging and the rejections you receive.

> In summary, rejecting rejection has four components:
>
> 1. Reject social impositions that feel wrong.
> 2. Reject the fear of being rejected from social groups when you follow your signs and personal directions or when you speak your mind with honesty and respect.
> 3. Understand that rejection by others often mirrors their ideas; so don't superimpose their ideas onto yourself.
> 4. Other people's rejection can be used as a "sign" and interpreted as the need to maintain what you have to offer and change the people to whom you are offering your "talents."

## 2. Expect Signs

Human cognition allows us to find more easily what we expect to find. When we expect signs, we need to remain vigilant and alert to catch even the slightest changes in our environment, thus the smallest signs. There are three main indicators that, when well observed, can guide you in the right directions:

1.  Feelings

2.  Physical reactions

3.  Events

An internal feeling is an unclear state that does not express a specific emotion or thought. It expresses a positive or negative sensation that is sometimes so minuscule that it is disregarded. It often needs magnification in order to be perceived.

We are all born with an internal "compass" that tells us what "feels good" and what "feels bad." Some people call this the conscience; others believe in the superconscious; and others yet would refer to a divine spirit. Most have a sense of their own "gut feelings," "intuition," or "instinct." Regardless of how we perceive the force that provides a sense of right or wrong, we are all endowed with it and should learn to follow it.

To do this, it is first imperative to distinguish internal dialogue (made of self-convictions, negative self-talk, and socially learned principles) from true inner feelings. Unless one is affected by a mental illness or pathology, we generally know if an action is right or wrong and are responsible for the decisions that follow.

Core beliefs are the innate certainties that are so engrained that they function automatically throughout your entire life. They constitute the pillars of your essence and are NOT to be confused with what society, family, or friends impose on you as a model. If you feel something is wrong, you will know it, despite what others say to persuade you. You will feel it with your inner sense of right and wrong and will most likely experience physical effects if you go against your core beliefs. A physical symptom is more evident and localized than a feeling and often manifests with enough strength to be noticed. Physical symptoms often indicate the root of a problem encountered in our lives or an unprocessed reaction to a stressful event.

Often you can discover deep meaning in a physical sign that is incessantly presented to you. The fuzzy logic behind reading physical signs requires some knowledge of physiology and a little intuition to accurately interpret the warnings they present. However, often we find that we actually intuitively know what the problems are as well as how to solve them.

Ignoring or suppressing feelings and symptoms is a bad strategy to control personal or social problems. In fact, feelings, symptoms, and events will regularly remind you of the things you need to do to re-establish harmony or balance, what steps you need to take to reach your ultimate goal(s), or to reconfirm that you are on your right personal track.

Signs are at times obvious and at other times very subtle. Understanding the signs in events requires an undistracted vigilant attention. Any distraction or beguilement is like a loud noise when trying to hear a whisper. When you finally hear the whisper or see the sign, you will often instinctively know if that event is significant or not, especially if it has been repeated a few times within a certain time-frame. Events as signs can be anything from a new encounter, an inspiring song that is heard at the right time, a conversation, thinking about someone only to run into him or her shortly after, an "accident" or "mistake," a slip of the tongue, an image, a dream, a person you keep meeting, etc. The best way to describe a meaningful event is that you will know when you encounter it. It will feel somehow significant and meaningful. The best way to explain how to make the most of a sign is to keep your eyes and heart open to it.

The important part of the sign is not the sign in itself but what you recognize in it. Pattern recognition can help infer meaning from signs. A famous example of a sign comes from the famous Swiss psychologist of the early 1900s, Carl Jung, who discovered the significance of meaningful coincidences or synchronicities while working on a patient. This patient was psychologically inaccessible, hyper-rational, and overly schematic in her way of thinking. After fruitless attempts to explore her emotional side, Jung resorted to hope that something completely unexpected would manifest to dissolve the intellec-

tual armor into which she was impris-
oned. While she was revealing a
dream in which she was given a
golden scarab, Jung suddenly heard a
tapping noise at the window, turned
around, walked towards it, and saw a
beetle, trying to get inside. Jung took
the beetle in his hands and gave it to the patient saying, "Here
is your golden scarab." This experience broke the ice and
opened a way to liberate the patient from her excessive ration-
alism.

### 3. Accept your Signs

Accepting and following the signs can sometimes be more
difficult than actually encountering and understanding them
because the logical conscious mind often gets in the way of our
subconscious. The conscious mind contains a database of
learned concepts that functions logically to filter information,
plan, calculate, and process details. Its qualities of precision
and prediction can complicate mental activity and often slow
down reaction times. Thinking of all possible outcomes of an
event can limit your ability to choose an action, especially
knowing that you're responsible for the outcome of your actions. The subconscious mind is much more powerful, working
holistically through feelings and intuition, to provide a general
sensation that can be ambiguous but most likely accurate. The
tendency to want clarity often renders people to suppress their
intuitive sense and focus on the logical understanding of things.

Signs are not always logical. They convey meaning
through interpretation and are not understood identically by
different people. Even the conscious and subconscious do not
always read the same meaning in a symbol. Be aware that the
conscious mind learns the meanings of symbols and could be
wrong in what it learned, whereas the subconscious is a symbolic processing unit, which accurately creates, uses, and responds to symbols and linguistic patterns. The Persona in you
can also interfere with the interpretation of signs and your
judgment when it comes to following them. Therefore, not only
is it important to overcome the Persona, but also recognize

that the subconscious is a much better tool to use to interpret the feelings, reactions, and events experienced.

Essentially, what the subconscious mind transmits to conscious awareness is symbolic in nature because it is the result of non-logical processes. In fact, personal belief systems direct future experiences through the forces of self-fulfilling prophecies and therefore confirm biased expectations. Furthermore, on a quantum level, we co-create our observation of reality through our subconscious energy outputs that stimulate the

---

The following are some common examples of physical reactions as signs:

♦ *Are you feeling sleepy, directionless, or physically ill?*

Your body may have fallen into a rest phase to force you to take time to recuperate and rebuild its rhythms.

♦ *Do your eyes burn often or do you have migraines that are encouraging you to close your eyes and completely isolate from the rest of the world?*

This could be an indication that your nervous system is overloaded and needs a temporary break to avoid further mental strain from focusing on one item of your life too intensively.

♦ *Are you experiencing an increase of weight or skin problems that reduce your attractiveness?*

Perhaps this is a strategy not to confront the effects that your beauty and attractiveness might procure, such as finding a meaningless relationship, being unfaithful, or being desired only for your physical qualities.

♦ *Does your child have an ear infection or inflammation?*

Maybe he/she needs some quiet space, with no noise, loud voices, or screaming. Also he/she might need less talking and more physical interaction.

♦ *Are you living with an important or debilitating disease?*

It is possible that you need to re-evaluate your priorities in life and concentrate on the very nature of the disease that is calling your attention.

---

+ *Do you often suffer from insomnia?*

It is possible that your conscious mind is overactive, for one reason or another. When the conscious mind's activity prevails over the body's natural functions and movements, insomnia might arise as a sign of alarm. You might need to be more physical and social.

+ Are you *feeling confused, blocked, overwhelmed, depressed, irritable, or unmotivated?*

Perhaps there is a Persona still within you providing you with a wrong attitude, a wrong stance, or a wrong sense of belonging, and generating some of the effects on the body mentioned earlier.

+ *Do you feel strong, youthful, motivated, and inspired?*

This may be an indication that what you're doing while these feelings take place is an enterprise you could engage in successfully.

---

occurrence of events. If you want to be in tune with the feelings, physical reactions, and events around you, then you must learn to be in tune with your subconscious.

To recognize conscious versus subconscious processes, consider what you are thinking when performing an action. Using "if, but, then, otherwise..." are clear indicators that the conscious mind is in full activity because it alone uses the rational and logical processing mechanisms to evaluate possibilities and prejudged actions to make prudent decisions. If you don't know why you did something, if you followed your gut feelings, or if you only have a vague sense of the event, then it is likely you used your subconscious.

Once you have begun dismantling your Persona, living in tune with your subconscious is much easier. It is like clearing away the background noise so you can hear your true inner voice. This will make it easier for you to accept what the signs in your life are telling you and to follow their messages.

## 4. Detect the Pattern

Major changes in your life will occur when you reject social impositions, as well as any fear of being rejected by them, when you learn to read meaningful and evocative signs through feelings, physical reactions, and events, and when you follow those signs as a trend. This will orientate you in a direction that you probably would not have expected. You may begin with confusion, uncertainty, and insecurity, but rest assured that this will certainly give you noticeable changes in your life. Self-trust, patience, and determination are required to follow this method.

To be able to constantly acknowledge your signs and detect a pattern in them requires wisdom. Wisdom does not consist of anticipating every possible consequence, for that would instead generate fear and anxiety. Wisdom is rather the foresight to accurately predict the outcome of events. It stems from a journey of previous experiences in which one remains willing to learn from achievements and mistakes, while having a relative certainty of the direction or flow of events. It is a bit like driving. Detecting the pattern of the street, you will adjust and direct your course while you proceed. Note that this happens "while you proceed," and not "before you proceed," since planning and conscious understanding is not part of this process.

Learning from your achievements and mistakes is not a difficult task. First, you must admit your achievements, thus self-condition to accomplish them again. Take satisfaction in your accomplishments, recognize the influences that facilitated them, and encourage yourself to follow them.

ACKNOWLEDGE YOUR ACCOMPLISHMENTS by continuing your efforts and by using positive reinforcement. This will reinforce the tendency to achieve again. For instance, after a strenuous period, reward yourself with some time off in a relaxing environment. Or, after having mastered a new skill, prize yourself with some food that makes your body (not your psyche) feel good.

Similarly, admit when a mistake is made, reflect on the forces that made it possible, and be swift in discontinuing the misguiding attitude. For instance, if you have lost the trust of some of your friends because you acted without consideration of their best interests, recognize this error, make up for it by rebuilding trusting relationships, and avoid making similar mistakes in the future.

When you are synchronous with your signs, you will better use experiences, both good and bad, as a compass to direct your way. Insights come with the deep understanding of your experiences and with the humbleness that allows them to reach you and speak to you.

## 5. Yield

As stated in Chapter 2, integrity is the congruence of internally consistent codes of attitudes, beliefs, and principles that lie in the inner core of your being. Integrity comes from the word *integer*, meaning "whole" or "complete," and implies an ability to be incorruptible because of a well-functioning congruent core. Trusting your inner core is what will provide you with the inner strength and direction to persevere with your goals.

### Your Inner Core

Here are some examples of how to adhere to your inner core:

+ Give voice to your thoughts even when they might seem strange to others.
+ Make choices based on what you feel is right, not what others believe.
+ Don't adopt rigid dogmas and don't impose your ideas on others.
+ Show others your path without criticizing theirs.
+ Focus on what you need, not what you want.
+ Behave in ways that are in harmony with your personal values.
+ Understand what you have, because you brought it into your own life.
+ Learn from your mistakes and from the meaningful signs in your life.

Yielding means to give space to your subconscious and allow determination to follow. It will provide you with the necessary courage to pursue the perceived goals, the strength to persevere, the compassion to help others along the way, and the prudence to be humble.

Yielding is the equivalent of letting go of the arrow you loaded on your bow. If your arrow is pointed in the right direction and the bow is tensed, all that is left is for you to let go. But why is letting go sometimes so hard?

*The most fundamental problem that affects humans is the inability to face uncertainty.*

## Skeptic Poison

Any good skeptic would tell you that there is no definite way to prove anything with 100% certainty. In fact, a good skeptic can disprove anything at any given time. Skeptics take things apart and then mock their malfunction. Whereas the actual root of the word "skeptic" means to look about and to consider, which could be constructive to analysis and objective observation, when something is passed through the eyes of a modern skeptic, it can become like a watch that has been dismantled and does not work any more. On the other hand, good observers consider the function of whole systems.

Skepticism is the cause of imposed ideas and attacks on different ways of thinking. Therefore, before being skeptical or suspicious about data, just remember that you need to have all the parts of the watch in an assembled and functional structure before you can form an opinion. Remember that a skeptical person is only trying to establish his or her own certainties by denying yours. Skepticism is a cynical and contemptuous symptom of "fear of uncertainty." It is a way to grip onto one's certainties, strongly denying and belittling the ones that do not fit an accepted scientific, ideological, or religious model.

What is perceived as "definite" philosophical, religious, or scientific truth often becomes disregarded as erroneous, incomplete, or preposterous some decade later. Just because most people believed the world was flat didn't mean it really was, and Galileo Galilei was killed for saying otherwise. Different ways of overcoming the absence of certainty have been in-

vented in the past, the most common being a religious or metaphysical belief, rivaled nowadays by the pompous attitude of
skepticism.

History is written by whoever wins the war and ideologies
are created and maintained by those who can impose their
point of view above others, often forcefully. It is important for
many skeptics, atheists, and agnostics to understand that for
most people, a belief, even when seemingly unrealistic, feels
better and is more constructive than uncertainty and nihilism.
A belief can give hope, and a relatively more comfortable state
of certainty. All beliefs should therefore be tolerated as personal certainties or subjective reference systems.

Prejudice, racism, distrust, and incredulity are defense
mechanisms against uncertainty. The more time it took to personally build a belief system, the more embedded and structured it will be, and the fiercer the battle will be to defend one's
certainties against others. Uncertainty can sometimes be so
discomforting and confusing that a person can feel pushed to
impose one's opinion on to others with violence and force. In
sum, if you want to understand the domain of this book, please
avoid skeptic attitudes and people with such thought processes,
for it will be of no help to you.

## Become W.I.S.E.R and R.E.A.D.Y

A common defense mechanism to conquer uncertainty is to
rely on what is already known and to remain within one's comfort zone. However, we are endowed with an innate curiosity
and a desire to follow ways that are not totally known; we are
pushed to venture into the realms of the indefinite in the search
for better understanding.

Though it might seem overly simplistic, the most straightforward and unbiased solution to uncertainty is to yield to
what you feel is stable, and to be integer to your perceived certainties, with extreme care not to impose them on others. The
perception of truth is highly subjective and relies on variable
logic.

You are encouraged to not only read through this advice
but to actually try it out. You can put into practice one tenet
at a time and ask yourself: have I been truthful to myself and

diligent enough in my actions? If you weren't, reflect on the social impositions and external influences that may have contributed to deviating you from what you felt was right.

W.I.S.E.R and R.E.A.D.Y are the attitudes you can adopt to challenge yourself into a better state of being. The attitude you adopt in your life is 100% your choice. You cannot blame nor praise anyone other than yourself for your attitude in life.

Attitude is the way you react to your environment and to the events around you. If you are truly open and sincere, you will be able to see the signs of your past mistakes and the indicators of your probable future. Only when you shine the light on the problem can you have the inspiration to adjust your stance. Once you have separated yourself from the power the Persona has over you, you can learn how to find your best future orientation and achieve the intentions you set for yourself.

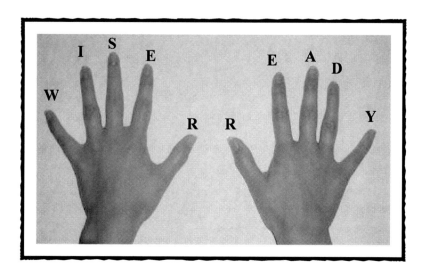

*"The real voyage of discovery consists not in seeking new landscapes, but in seeing with new eyes."*

— *Marcel Proust*

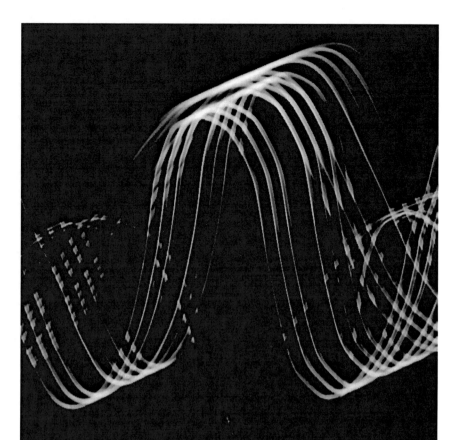

# Chapter 7
# Your Resonant
# Way

*"If you learn only methods,*
*you'll be tied to your methods,*
*but if you learn principles you*
*can devise your own methods."*
— *Ralph Waldo Emerson*

After clarifying and working through your pending doubts and your past rejections, you might have had a glimpse that your past attitudes have contributed to shape the person you have become and ultimately your destiny. Now a new attitude is needed to find what lies ahead. As a Chinese saying goes, *"If you want to see what is ahead, look at what is behind, because it is one's past conduct that will influence future events."*

With the exercises of Chapter 5, we learn that as long as we maintain the wrong stance or live in the wrong environment, pending problems and confusions are not solved because we have no energy to move forward. Moving forward is the essence of our evolution. The French philosopher Henri Bergson, in his 1907 book *Creative Evolution*[14], introduced the concept of *Élan vital*, or vital force, as being a possible core or "engine" for evolution and motivation. Essentially, Bergson believed the evolutionary urge for mankind is the impulse to use one's *will* to create, to invent, to discover, and to establish a reality. We receive more energy when motivated and we are compelled to act when we feel part of a greater whole. Furthermore, our sense of belonging derives from a process of *identification*, which takes place psychologically and physically.

## Identification and Resonance

Psychologically, identification occurs when we attribute to ourselves the characteristics and qualities of another person or group of people. When we think similarly, and enjoy being in each other's company, we associate with that person or group and make of them part of our identity. We are our team, our group, our society, our nation. When we identify and embrace the group, we strive for the well-being of that group. This goes back to the concept of needing a sense of belonging mentioned in Chapter 1.

Physically, identification corresponds to a very specific phenomenon: *physical resonance*. Resonance is literally a reinforcement and intensification of vibrations. If you take two tuning forks of the same frequency, striking one will cause the other to vibrate because of their similar shape. Similarly, a precise physiological process causes empathy between you and another person, situation, or group of people. When you feel a good sensation in regards to a given condition, it is because this vibration strikes your natural frequency, makes it resonate, and produces energy. The result is a feeling of being energized and in a state of well-being

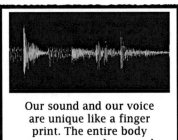

Our sound and our voice are unique like a finger print. The entire body creates a complex sound through the agitation of the atoms that compose our cells.

When vibrations that are different from your natural one are imposed on you, no resonance is produced and no sense of goal or direction emerges. A chronic absence of identification or resonance causes lower energy levels, no sense of involvement, and reduced activity of the immune and endocrine systems. Depression and a weak body-mind configuration also follow. Similarly, resonances based on selfish goals and desires will generate quick flares of pleasure that swiftly dissolve with residual feelings of gloominess and dissatisfaction.

In 1925, the Russian bioelectronics engineer Georges Lakhovsky[15] found that all living cells (people, plants, bacteria, and so on) possess the attributes normally associated with electronic resonators. In fact, cells can be seen as microscopic oscillating circuits capable of emitting and absorbing radiations of very high frequencies, like microscopic tuning forks. These oscillating circuits, when supplied with energy from an external source, are set in vibration and oscillate at their natural frequency.

According to the well-known researchers Stewart Hameroff and Roger Penrose[16], these vibrations might be transmitted by the cytoplasma of our cells, the gel-like substance in which cell organs and nucleus are held. This cytoplasma is made of a skeleton that consists of microtubular filaments. These filaments work as antennas for the transmission of consciousness. Just like an antenna can capture radio signals due to its shape and orientation, the cytoskeleton's components (the filaments) could be the basic units of biological and mental processing rather than the neurons. In other words, our subconscious mind operates through our entire body, at the cellular level, rather than only at a neuronal level (in the brain).

Chapter 4 described the adaptation and plasticity of neural networks. There is an equivalent network at the cellular level, not made of neurons but of the filaments called *microtubules*. These are responsible for the transfer of chemical information in the structural network of the cell's main constituent, the cytoplasm, and their malfunction has been associated with cancer. Neurons are thus for the brain and conscious mind what microtubules are for all cells and for the subconscious.

Atomic vibration determines the state of resonance that our body emits.

Every cell and atom in our body produces a sound called thermal noise. This sound is your fundamental note; the natural, complex sound you produce when the atoms of your 100 trillion cells vibrate together in unison. When other people, environments, or situations emit a similar "vibration," you will immediately feel a sense of internal stimulation, excitement, animation, and purpose. You won't need to rationalize what is good or most appropriate to follow; you will physically know in an instant. This is your body telling you that a similar wave is striking you! This resonant wave invigorates and directs you, it pushes you to be involved and committed to an action, and it gives you the drive to achieve your goals. It is the signal that you are on the right track.

Identification gives you purpose and the energy to accomplish your goals. It corresponds to a detectable arousal and signal that you can literally put to the test and track in order to know what gives stimulation and what does not. Even the people around you will notice the change in you when you yield to your natural resonances. They will notice that you look better, younger, more energized, and happier. Your work productivity will increase, your motivation will be higher, you will feel healthier, and you will no longer feel hindered by the challenges you face. Though there are laboratory instruments that can tell you when you are aroused or stimulated by something and when you are not, you can simply use your body to feel your resonances.

If you followed the exercises of this book so far, you have probably experienced a brief but insightful detachment from previous social and self-imposed conditioning. When you are detached from your biased mind, your identification is more likely to be the correct one. If the Persona still resides in you with strength, or begins to germinate again, it is possible that your thinking network will create too much noise for you to hear the subtleties of the resonances within you. If you changed your stance and moved away, even if for a short time, from past social conditioning, you can begin to practice reading and accepting signs, and identifying which event, person, or goal gives you arousal, energy, and motivation.

The exercises of this book will have also briefly taught you how to recognize patterns. You will be able to notice similarities in the situations that stimulate more enthusiasm and inspiration in you. It is at this point that the 5 External Attitudes of Chapter 6 really come into play. Follow the signs and be R.E.A.D.Y. to proceed with the investigation of your resonant path!

Use a notebook to take note of what gives you arousal and encourages you to be more involved. While meeting people, watching a movie, traveling to another city or country, reading a book, listening to a song, or having ideas, always pay attention to the things that give you happiness and enthusiasm. Over the next few months, see if you can recognize the resonant pattern that best suits you. Finding your resonance takes time, but if you really don't find anything interesting in your surroundings or anything that gives you a feeling of excitement, try to change your environment and take note of the effects this has on you.

## *Resonant Wave Patterns*

Signs and waves of resonance can be summarized and simplified into 8 fundamental patterns. These resonant wave patterns represent 8 general manifestations of life and are not only wave archetypes, but also representative expressions of specific phenomena on a larger scale. The model of waves used here is based on the theory of the *Holonomic Brain*[17] according to the neuroscientist Karl Pribram, and the fact that our perception of the environment is received in general impressions or *Gestalts*.

Gestalts are general impressions of the reality we experience. When we feel completely integrated and satisfied with something in our lives, we know through insight that something resonates with us and makes us feel good. "Good" does not merely refer to a simple feeling of well-being, but is a state where we should see our "True North," our real orientation, our way. When we feel fulfilled and satisfied beyond our normal threshold, when we resonate like a string of a violin stroked with a perfect movement, and when we know that what we are doing is the right thing, we are experiencing resonance.

This model presents 8 major Resonant Wave Patterns with which people tend to resonate. Take the time to get to know the different patterns and try to identify the one that resonates with you. Though we may be inclined to think there is more than one that resonates at different times in our lives, there is only one that can vibrate to the natural tune of your cells. Knowing which one resonates will help you sense the direction of your inner compass, the path of life you were meant to walk.

When standing in the middle of a forest, there are many paths one can take. Recognizing where your True North is will help you use your inner compass to find the path that best suits you. Though the compass can point in the direction, the decision to follow it remains yours.

## 0. The Soothing Wave

The Soothing Wave resonates with you if you feel excited and happy by helping others to relax and recuperate, or if you feel the need to nurture, look after, raise, foster, and care for other people or groups, asking for nothing in return. If you enjoy promoting development through wise encouragement, patience, and company, and if you find joy in being a moral support and a reservoir of good examples, beyond the responsibilities of a loving parent, then you resonate with the Soothing Wave. People who resonate with this wave find satisfaction in enjoying purity of spirit, honesty, and morality, and promoting the same in other people, thus effectively changing people's lives.

*The Soothing Wave finds comfort in comforting.*

## 1. The Impacting Wave

If you feel energized and fulfilled when you are physically active, when you are impacting others, and when you are able to stir, move, or lead others to important decisions, then you resonate with the Impacting Wave. The Impacting Wave makes you feel motivated by motivating others and pushing them to be stronger and fitter, to better survive their environment, and to overcome their problems. This wave is perceived in challenging, intense, and impactful situations; it is the direct opposite of comfort, laziness, and calm. Those who resonate with the Impacting Wave motivate others through their impact.

*The Impacting Wave finds motivation in motivating.*

## 2. The Synchronizing Wave

If you feel invigorated and blissful when you have time to meditate and find solutions for other people's problems with the help of your intuition and insight, then you resonate with the Synchronizing Wave. Those who resonate with this wave find happiness in comforting others, in helping others overcome their personal obstacles, and providing others with mental and physical health. A true interest in humanism, psychology, anthropology, and other social sciences generally emerges from the genuine care for other people's well-being and peace of mind.

*The Synchronizing Wave finds serenity in giving inner peace.*

### 3. The Standing Wave

If you feel devoted to maintaining structures and providing material sustenance to the members of your family or a larger group, providing funding or resources for good projects, finding pleasure in maintaining and managing assets, structures, and money, or are interested in economy, investments, properties, and landscapes, then you resonate with the Standing Wave. Inner satisfaction is achieved by helping others with supplies of basic needs for survival, material goods, or economical support.

*The Standing Wave finds stability in stabilizing others.*

### 4. The Rising Wave

The Rising Wave resonates well with you if you get energy and joy from helping others through education, learning, self-improvement, organization, self-discipline, and overall achievement. A continuous drive to refine and clarify, pay attention to details, and provide structure and order is generated by the Rising Wave.

*The Rising Wave finds assurance in giving certitude to others.*

### 5. The Expanding Wave

Those who resonate with the Expanding Wave feel excited and jovial in social networks. If you enjoy maintaining public relations, bringing people together, publicizing information, reporting to large numbers of people, or organizing meetings, encounters, events, and gatherings, then you resonate with the Expanding Wave. By unifying and grouping people, you can provide a thriving environment for brainstorming and creativity, and will find satisfaction in other people's pleasure.

*The Expanding Wave finds wholeness in creating wholes.*

### 6. The Yielding Wave

If studying the path of least resistance and striving for equilibrium in life motivate you, and if you find gratification in being compliant and acquiescent with others, then you resonate with the Yielding Wave. Those who resonate with this wave are drawn to knowledge acquisition, enjoy multitasking, are interested in research and information, and feel moved by issues related to life and liveliness. If you feel the urge to contribute to the equilibrium of the environment developing a deeper understanding of the way things are, or using your problem-solving techniques to find resolution to current issues, then the Yielding Wave is resonating with you.

*The Yielding Wave finds balance in balancing.*

## 7. The Intensifying Wave

If you are driven by constructing, inventing, and putting elements together to form new creations and innovations, or if you find joy in pushing the limits of new enlightening methodologies, then you resonate with the Intensifying Wave. Those who resonate with this wave are interested in improving all disciplines of research and development, as well as multidisciplinary studies, integration, holism, and structural designs of practical systems of living from a leadership position. The purpose is to bring together and push forward.

*The Intensifying Wave finds inspiration in inspiring.*

## *Determining Your Goal*

When you follow your inner compass and take note of what resonates in you, ideas and opportunities will arise. Remember that signs are at times obvious and at other times very subtle. You need to be W.I.S.E.R and mentally clear of the mental noise the Persona can cause so you can hear the subtleties of the signs life presents you. Similarly, when you remain R.E.A.D.Y, you will be able to detect the pattern of your signs and better use your inner compass to direct your way.

You are the only one who ultimately knows how to determine what is best for you. As long as you follow your fascination, your passion, your inspiration, and your excitement, you will find what it is you're looking for. Sometimes, a great idea will come to you in a dream, while going about your daily routine, while trying to solve a problem, or in a conversation. Opportunities may arise while waiting for the bus, during a phone call, or while speaking to friends and colleagues.

Frequently, your goal will appear when you least expect it. It may happen that you will have to grab an idea or opportunity quickly while you can, while other times you will find yourself doing what it is you were born to do without even realizing it, only noticing much later all the positive changes in you. Essentially, when you remain W.I.S.E.R, R.E.A.D.Y, and clear of the Persona, your inner compass will naturally point due North because resonant wave patterns are like the magnetic pull of the poles.

However, if the Persona is still strong in you, it may reject this notion as inconsequential, impossible, or simply not suitable for you. The Persona can act like a blockage to the natural magnetic field that tells you where your inner compass should point. Your challenge is to rise above the Persona and get in touch with your natural resonance. Follow the signs and identify your true nature so that you can do what you were really born to do.

## Assessing the Quality of Your Goals

Throughout this book, purpose, intention, and ultimate objectives have been assessed. Whereas the Persona's focus is on reconfirming "rules of thought" to ensure its existence, persistence, and reproduction, the subconscious will aim at what is best for you.

Included in your subconscious' objectives are your health, your well-being, and your happiness, and the best way for it to achieve this is when it is in harmony with the external environment. Your subconscious will take into account your inborn talents, natural abilities, and innate capacities without ever making you feel incomplete, unsatisfied, or as though your

Every time you resonate with a specific goal, reflect on the following questions to see if your inner arousal is a selfless and purposeful one:

♦ Are your goals *really* making you involved, interested, and excited?

♦ Are your goals *really* contributing to a greater good?

♦ Are your goals *really* beneficial to you and to others?

goals were unattainable. Furthermore, the more you achieve a sense of belonging, approach life with the right attitude, and are motivated by what you can do for others, the more all-encompassing your goals will be.

Notice that none of the questions to assess your goal refer to feasibility or likelihood of accomplishment. Anything that you truly resonate with at a cellular level can be achieved if you fall into your natural state and if you are creative in finding a way past the barriers your conscious mind can create.

Following these guidelines will make your new path in life an awakened one, full of exciting events that contribute to the greater scheme of things. In fact, with the help of the following chapter, you will learn how to take your goal and expand it to aim higher, reaching a bigger population, and becoming more long-lasting in its effects. An ultimate purpose in life should not remain a selfish one, but should extend as far and wide as possible. The more we all think of others, the closer we get to becoming a harmonious whole, just like each individual cell which functions synchronously with the entire organism.

*"The meaning of our existence
is not invented by ourselves,
but rather detected."*

— *Viktor Frankl*

# Chapter 8
# Encompassing
# Everything
# Under the Sun

*"Vision without action is a daydream. Action without vision is a nightmare."*
    —*Japanese Proverb*

A strong motivation derives from the notion of having a future orientation, a future existence. Unfortunately, social conditioning dehumanizes us to the point that we have no enthusiasm, a poor sense of belonging, and an inability to resonate with what innately brings us joy and energy. Our dissatisfaction with life encourages us to acquire and maintain a Persona, like millions of other people. However, realizing that this phenomenon has been intensifying exponentially with modern society can shed light on how past civilizations have coped with their evolutionary glitch.

## Striving to be More than Human

Throughout history, humans quickly understood that life in the physical body is temporary; death is inevitable. In fact, the fear of death seems to be the most primary of all fears. The common reaction to the thought of death procures emotions ranging from intense fear to constant anxiety. Future existence or continuation was, and still is, a reason for a will to live. In his book, *The Denial of Death*[18], Ernst Becker explains how human culture and civilization are driven by the intense need to exorcise death anxieties through the creation of systems that allow survival. In an attempt to defend against death, we need to feel as if we have the potential to become something that is greater and longer lasting. Although the survival of one's family, clan, and species is a cellular and instinctive drive, we also need to know that we can become more than human, more than mortal. We therefore become creative. We produce art that will last longer than our bodies, create long-lasting enterprises, think of new philosophies, make scientific discoveries, and do anything memorable that will put our existence into continuation. These efforts are all in the attempt of having extra-corporeal survival: existing beyond the natural death of the physical body.

An effort or strong desire to survive as more than human activates psycho-endocrine responses that can actually change the mood and psychological state of a person. As described in Chapter 2, tearing our focus away from what is most important in life obstructs the process of our becoming something great; this can lead to mental instability and possibly be the seed for mental illness. According to Becker, stopping the drive for immortality, which he defines as the Hero System, creates a sense of insignificance, lack of will, depression, discouragement, purposelessness, and anxiety. The memento of one's death and the failure of one's "heroism" simultaneously cause a lack of well-being in life and an absence of direction.

When everything good and worth fighting for disappears, the sense of continuation and our internal motivation collapses, and with it our élan vital or life drive. By accepting the belief that you can't achieve peak experiences, or that you have nothing exceptional to strive for, you are accepting death. By accepting this way of thinking, you abdicate your natural right to become stronger and better. By immersing in the small insignificant details in life, you no longer look at the bigger, more important picture. You no longer see your purpose in life because you remain focused on bills, brand names, petty conflicts, or TV shows. Rather than having purposeful and important future orientations, life goals become centered on seeking material goods, social acknowledgement, or status. It is only when we believe that there is something more to life that we can believe in a greater goal to achieve: a higher purpose.

## What is Killing the Hero System?

Psychologists Sheldon Solomon, Jeff Greenberg, and Tom Pyszczynski[19] discovered that when people are subconsciously reminded of their own death, they tend to be harsher in judgment and punishment or more hostile towards people who possess different ideologies than themselves, while becoming more fraternal with members of their own group. In other words, the subconscious perception of death creates an overall feeling of mortality, inferiority, and an impulse to separate from individuals with unfamiliar ideologies, while strengthening the solidarity within the clan or in-group. This phenomenon helps leaders maintain obedient control over their population as well as their loyalty to willingly risk their life for their land.

## Mental Control with Death Reminders

The perception of death presents a small sense of disorientation resulting in high suggestibility. The fear of death and metaphysical or after-life punishment was a tool of domination that lasted for thousands of years. Many cultures throughout history have understood the effect that reminders of death can have on people. Examples include the Ancient Aztecs with their representation of the skeleton-like god of sacrifice Michlantenluchi, the Tibetans with their representation of the demon of death, the Indian cults of Shiva, and the Catholic Church and its use of the crucifix. Extensive use of such symbology was frequently used to control the population's behavior through fear, and is still used today. Reminders of death in the form of skulls, bones, crucifixes, or skeletons create a subconscious motivation to stick to the clan, and instill a sense of mortality and enhanced suggestibility.

Modern society uses an equivalent of the death reminder: the news in the media. The information we receive everyday, from television, magazines, newspapers, or radio are continuously overflowing with reminders of death. Whether we are exposed to scenes of death and violence, or reminded of our mortality through talks of disease and poor standards of living, the media persistently hounds us. Death reminders keep us in a state of depression, dissatisfaction, frustration, and feeling unable to make the necessary changes to improve our lives. This is why we strongly advise you to avoid this sort of information while reading this book. Detach yourself from social conditioning when you challenge yourself to a better life. Seek life, not death.

## Where are the True Heroes?

Ernst Becker sees an additional fatal blow to the Hero System in the advent of modern materialistic ways of living. Reducing life and nature to meaningless structures, over which we have no control, and diminishing human beings to nothing more than thinking animals, gives little room for the Hero in us. When one's Hero System and one's sense of purpose has been destroyed, the last defense one has against the fear of mortality is the creation of an illusory world made of fake heroic systems like idols, movie stars, pin-ups, and other celebrities. We look to celebrities to be our "heroes" because they are wealthy or famous, when we should actually be looking for examples of heroes that reflect higher qualities in humans, such as strength, purity, uprightness, and good judgment.

Whereas our heroes should contribute meaningfully, purposefully, and significantly to the world, social conditioning tries to maintain our focus on the most basic desires, without encouraging us to contribute to something eternal and immortal. In fact, the media will attempt to distract us further by encouraging us to live vicariously through the lives of others through magazine articles about celebrities' petty problems or reality television programs about people's trivial behavior. The conditioning influences of our society make us feel small and focused on the insignificant details of our lives.

## *Continuation is Motivation, Motivation is Continuation*

Life is the big picture. Life is seen through continuation and projection into the future, through expansion and cooperation, through understanding and personal motivation. The larger your perception of the world, the better your understanding is of the meaning of Life Continuation.

To enlarge your perception, try the following exercises. The goal of these exercises is to set your attention outward to the world around you instead of the internal, introspective world. Instead of focusing on the tiny details of your life, begin thinking about the greater whole and how your actions can benefit the greater good. The experience of thinking big is enlightening. Your subconscious mind does not differentiate between imagined and "real." The act of merging into a bigger state is perceived by your subconscious as being bigger, and it opens the doors to act towards a larger goal.

Once you have had glimpses of what your consciousness is without the constant effect of a Persona, with the exercises of Chapter 5, you should be in a higher level of understanding. You may have sporadic episodes of perceptions that are completely merged with your environment, feeling as though your external surroundings are part of your senses. You should have the ability to think in terms of great deeds for a larger group of people, and be able to find the future orientation that best resonates with you, as described in Chapter 7. With a fresh start and a clear target, you are now able to learn the skills to properly shoot your arrows.

## *Mind-Opening Exercises*

### 1. Looking above and beyond

The mind is a remarkable tool when you harness its abilities. If you were to consider your imaginary three-dimensional structure as your goal, imagine what you can achieve when you stretch it and apply it to a greater area. This is how you can take action for the benefit of the collective.

1. Touch the tips of your index fingers in front of your eyes at a distance of about 20 cm or 8 inches away from your nose.
2. Bring them slowly closer, keeping your eyes focused on a distant point above and beyond your fingers.
3. Eventually, you will see a sausage-like shape, created by the tips of both your fingers.

   You can't see it if you focus on what's right in front of you, but *it's amazing what you can discover when your vision is broad.*

## 2. Expanding your vision

1. Look in front of you and take note of what you are looking at.
2. Select a very precise spot in front of you not greater than the tip of a needle.
3. Slowly enlarge your focal point to a space of about 10 cm or 4 inches in diameter.
4. Keep enlarging until your center of attention reaches 1 meter or 1 yard in diameter.
5. Keep enlarging slowly but steadily until your focus reaches what you perceive as 10 meters or 11 yards in diameter.
6. Keep enlarging until the diameter is as large as a big building.
7. Keep enlarging until the diameter is as large as your entire city.
8. Keep enlarging until the diameter is as large as your entire country.
9. Keep enlarging until the diameter is as large as your entire continent.
10. Keep enlarging until the diameter is as large as the entire Earth.
11. Maintain the last state for 5 minutes, and then slowly and progressively come back, stage-by-stage, to the starting point.
12. Repeat this twice and take note of your new perceptions and feelings.

*Those who achieve great flexibility of mind can gain new insights when they truly see the bigger picture.*

## *A Broader Mind, A Broader Heart*

Only through conditioning and your compliance can your imagination disappear and your attitude become negative. Hu-

## 3. Building and expanding

1. Pick a spot relatively close to you in mid-air to look at as your focal point. Be sure that what you are looking at is not in relation to any object, it should be empty space.
2. While maintaining the first point, pick another one in mid-air.
3. While maintaining the first two points, pick another one.
4. Continue until you have six points in total.
5. You have now a three-dimensional imagined structure made of your points in mid-air. Take the imagined structure with your hands and start moving it. Move it to your left. Move it to your right. Stretch it. Compress it. Spin it around.
6. When you feel comfortable with this, try enlarging your imagined structure slowly and progressively as you did in the previous exercise.

*Give your mind the chance and your imagination will fly. A lack of imagination is your mind's worst limitation.*

man beings have a natural instinct to survive and expand as a group, but through conditioning they can be tricked into losing their creativity, their positive attitude, and their sense of belonging.

When you connect the power of an unbiased mind to the strength of pure resonance, the possibilities are vast. An expanded awareness and reverberation of the environment coupled with a diminished rational superimposition of a biased Persona will leave you more alert to the signs that guide you in the right directions. The more you approach life with the right outlook, the better your stance will be, the more energy and dedication you will have, and the better your performance abilities will be when you do what you were born to do. It is

your attitude that really provides you with the motivation you
need to achieve.

Now that you have initiated the process of disconnecting
your Persona in Chapter 5, learned to exercise your inner compass in Chapter 6, followed your feelings to what resonates with
you in Chapter 7, and investigated the scope of expanded perception with the "mind-opening" exercises of this chapter, you
are ready to move into action. The next step is to reflect on targets that encompass more than your current vision does.

When your natural inner core really resonates with your
goal, your future orientation becomes clear and your motivation rises exponentially. People who are truly motivated find
they have much more energy, can achieve their tasks in less
time and with more inspiration than before, and find great happiness in the things they do. This section is meant to encourage
you, once you have found the right resonance and goal, to expand this to a greater population than you otherwise would
have.

Imagine your sole purpose in
life was to garden, to cultivate
plants and produce. Though
you could plant a vegetable
garden in your yard, focusing
only on yourself, you will feel
better if you plant enough there
for your family. You may even
gain a sense of pride when you see them enjoying what you
have cultivated. Knowing that your family has the sustenance
they need may be rewarding, but there is certainly room for
more in your life. If you expand this small garden to a farm,
you could provide for your entire community. Many more people will be grateful for your involvement in their well-being,
making you feel appreciated, valued, and motivated. But if you
were to add ingenuity to your gardening skills, you could also
extend your produce to satisfy those in need of nutrition in an
entire nation, or have your services impact people in future
generations.

Although it is acceptable to be content with what you
have, the more your vision builds and expands on what you

already have and do, the more drive you will have to pursue your goals. In the end, the objective to obtaining greater goals is to expand your vision in space (to a larger population) and time (aiming at long-term impacts). When you move higher on the Life Goal Scale, your accomplishments will feel more rewarding and longer lasting.

## *The Life Goal Scale*

If we were to graph the intensity of motivation, the two main factors to consider would be intention and energy. The more one's intention is outward-focused and all-encompassing, aiming at a greater number of people, at the greater good, the higher it can be plotted on the scale. Similarly, the more one's goal involves giving positive influence to others, the higher it can be plotted on the scale; as opposed to taking energy from others, which would be lower on the scale.

With the help of the descriptions below, you can easily plot where people fluctuate on the Life Goal Scale and where you would like to be with your future actions. This scale is subjective, dependent on your honest opinions about yourself. Only when you know where you stand can you then find the resonant way you should use as a model to strive for a higher purpose.

The purpose of this scale is to challenge yourself to strive a little higher than what you normally think you are capable of. When you have something to aim for, you become more energized and motivated. One of the ways to push one's self further is to project with intention and feasibility the activity that you will perform. Project every detail of your activity, the location where it takes place, the people involved, the feelings elicited… every available detail. Envision a scene that encompasses more than your personal goal; orient towards a higher purpose. Only when you act towards achieving those tasks can you actualize your goal.

**100:** This level is an extraordinary state of efficiency in an all-encompassing goal and a continuous creative influence on one's environment. Long-lasting effects on people's culture that are devoid of misinterpretations that could lead to war or conflicts, stem from this level, given the higher understanding of human nature. Buddha Gautama, Confucius, and the Chinese emperor Huang Di, who largely contributed to Asian medicine and philosophy, are good examples of this level on the Life Goal Scale.

**80:** This is a state in which the life goal reaches far beyond the self, with a vision that strongly and incessantly pushes towards the achievement of a better humanity. It is a highly important goal with unambiguous awareness of its influential effects over a large population for an extended period of time. Isaac Newton, Nikola Tesla, Mahatma Gandhi, Martin Luther King, Jr., and the Dalai Lama would be examples of people at this level.

**60:** At this point, the future orientation or goal extends to a much larger group than one's community. The desire is to improve one's self to advance in society, while contributing to a larger population with highly positive influences.

**40:** This is a general condition of personal success, sometimes accompanied by slight boredom and indifference for the greater surroundings. Efforts are focused on trying to obtain what's possible for one's self, one's family, and one's in-group (friends and community).

**20:** This is a state of struggle caused by a collapse of the Hero System, in which one's energy is focused on maintaining the current level of survival by fighting one's way through the system. Intention is mainly focused on the problems that caused self-collapse and the attempt to solve them. The interest is directed to one's own satisfaction of immediate needs and does not or cannot extend fully to the family or others. This level includes people struggling to maintain or get a job or career.

**0:** This is a state of hermitage and seclusion. In this state, a person does not take anything and does not give anything to anyone. It is a state of detachment from the world or mere selfishness in providing only enough for the self.

**-20:** This level represents the group of people who take from others without giving in return. Though this level includes children who are not yet able to contribute to society and those with innate mental disabilities, it also includes those living off social welfare when actually physically and mentally able to work, those living off parent's pension or assets, or those having disinterest in work and social contributions of any kind. This level also includes those who commit small crimes, because they are essentially taking from others.

**-40:** Any mental illness (anorexia, schizophrenia, psychoses, etc.) not accompanied by a biological cause, consciously or subconsciously maintained to attract energy from others onto themselves is included in this level. People at this level require attention, energy, and care from others to the point of draining those who care for them and making the caretakers unable to achieve their own personal life goals.

**-60:** This level includes any state of mental illness and extreme hopelessness, without serious organic causes, as well as those who attempt or commit suicide. This is a state where a person creates a permanent influence on the members of the family or clan that remain alive and acts as a source of sufferance for others. Their behavior is a punishment for the living.

**-80:** This level represents any mental state that drives a human being to harm or commit evil upon other living beings (i.e. serious criminal activity). This level includes taking the life of innocent beings on a premeditated basis, as well as any scientist who intentionally develops tools for destruction like the

100
80
60
40
20
0
-20
-40
-60
-80
-100

**The Life Goal Scale**

Take a look at this scale and keep in it mind when setting your goals. Be as honest and objective with yourself as possible. Aim too high and you may be setting yourself up for disappointment; aim too low and you may be limiting yourself.

atomic bomb, biological weapons, and harmful chemicals.

**-100:** This is the ultimate state of Life Goal destruction with a strong influence on the masses, where energy and resources are taken from others on a large scale with no sense of morals, compassion, empathy, or remorse. Extreme forms of physical violence to any living being, or the removal of the most basic survival needs of large populations would be included in this level. The action and the consequences of such deeds of most dictators like Mao, Stalin, Hitler, and Pol Pot are major manifestations of this level.

Once you have placed yourself and your ambitions on the Life Goal Scale, you can better understand where your targets lie and figure out how to achieve your goals. So far, the activities in this book were mere preparations for the actions you can embrace, and the biggest challenges still lie ahead of you. The bigger the goals, the bigger the challenge, but if you meet the challenge, you can reach the peak of your performance abilities.

Unfortunately, many people are limited by their fears. Whether it be the fear of responsibility that comes with success, the fear of shame that comes with failure, or the fear of rejection that comes with ambitious endeavors, it is generally fear that limits a person's ability to achieve great deeds.

## *Meet the Challenge*

Overcoming your flaws and fears opens you to become extraordinary, to the point of serving as a source of inspiration for others. As the Chinese saying of Lao Tzu goes, "*Conquering others takes force, but conquering yourself is true strength.*"

### *Overcoming your fears allows you to harness your way.*

Conquering fear, especially the fear of death, is the main challenge of any hero in well-known sagas, poems, stories, and tales. Even the act of slaying a dragon represents the act of mastering the functions of the part of the brain that we have common with reptiles: the *Reptilian brain*. The Reptilian brain, or R-complex, constitutes a relic of our prehistoric past. It harbors instinctive, preconscious behavior, involuntary reflexes, and automatic activities such as the control of respiratory, cardiac, and basic vital functions.

Unfamiliar experiences, along with the outcomes we cannot know or predict, can cause a reaction of fear and elicit a general response of alertness in the R-Complex. When the biased part of our conscious mind or Persona tries to solve problems that have too many unknown variables, strong signs of stress arise. Change, unprecedented experiences, and unfamiliar circumstances or conditions in which outcomes are unclear can cause deep feelings of uncertainty and stress.

As discussed in Chapter 2, we often decide to remain in a situation that is undesired because we are afraid of our unknown, possible future. Emotional or psychological stress is the effect of part of our conscious mind being overwhelmed by its inability to predict possible outcomes and provide a clear, safe direction. First, signs of tension and fatigue are manifested, which are then followed by a subconscious activation of the R-complex. This is the critical moment that must be harnessed! This is where we often fail.

When the conscious mind is overwhelmed, the R-complex takes over, thus promoting alertness, vigilance, and a faster reactivity, along with a sense of restlessness and discomfort. A correct amount of stress or tension is necessary to maintain healthy energetic behavior. When stress or tension is too high or too low, states of decompensation arise. For instance, an overly predictable life breeds boredom, depression, and dullness, whereas a life that is too unpredictable propagates disorientation, anxiety, and angst. *Eustress* is the correct amount of stress or "unpredictability" needed for a sense of fulfillment and to meet the challenges of life. To quote Viktor Frankl,

> *"What a man actually needs is not a tensionless state but rather the striving and struggling for some goal worthy of him. What he needs is not the discharge of tension at any cost, but the call of a potential meaning waiting to be fulfilled by him."*[20]

Though chronic stress and persistent fear can cause health problems, the modern solution of seeking stress-free and over-comfortable lives through a lack of challenge, overmedication, alcohol, drugs, and problem-avoidance is a flawed solution. Life is full of problems and we need to be aware of and prepare for that. In your life, you would have probably had at least one experience of the "grip" of fear. But did ever you stop to analyze it or to understand it? Probably not.

The state of gripping fear causes the body to shut down the thinking mind and redirects all the energy to cellular survival. When reacting to a great threat, the body becomes tightly clenched. It is the "gripping" contraction of body tissues that then becomes associated with the event of fear. When you begin to understand the mechanisms that function behind stress and fear, you will understand how you can harness physical tension to provide you the vigor and drive to propel you forward. This is the tension you need to shoot your arrows so that you can hit your target.

In response to real, imagined, or unidentified threats, the body responds with a temporary stiffness of the tissues. Every significantly fearsome event in the past has therefore created a memory of tensions, almost like a "armor," in the specific parts of the body that were affected by the fear. These body parts now have a limited flow of electrical energy, lymph, and blood along the tightened tissues. However, if you learn to release all the tension in your tissues by accepting a challenge, an "electric surge" from your body can initiate a state of enhanced vigor. The body will not provide you with energy unless there is a good prospect to use it.

The best way to prepare for a challenge is to keep in mind that *any fear of failure creates a stop in your cellular continuum of energy.*

Fear of failure impedes your natural way. When a fear arises (uncertainty, anxiety, fear of failure, etc.), the best option you have is to let it come and to accept the challenge. Do not listen to your self-talk or believe projections of possible future outcomes. Let the fear show and then give space to your R-complex. Avoid any attempt to rationalize the fear or problem; avoid conceptualization and logical thinking processes. Let your primitive brain engage in the challenge. Once the challenge is perceived, higher strength and determination

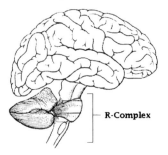

R-Complex

will flow. When you perceive a fear, wait for the tension to manifest. When the tension becomes marked, instead of pulling back and avoiding the engagement with the problem you are facing, yield and let your subconscious mind take control.

You can similarly harness this natural survival mechanism by meeting daily challenges. Every time you doubt yourself, push yourself a little further and notice your accomplishments. Do you remember a time when you had a fear of failure? What did you do? What happened to you? What was the outcome of your fear?

Notice that each time you push yourself a little further, you achieve much more than you expected. Sometimes after achieving what you did not expect to achieve, you might realize how different your opinion was previously in regards to what you considered possible or impossible. Sometimes you will encounter failure, but if you never try, you will have no chance of being successful.

Like a spring, stress causes tension that can bounce back with great force if properly released. A lack of tension leaves a spring to rust from disuse. Too much chronic tension becomes tiresome to hold and can bounce back at inappropriate moments, causing more harm than good. Fear, stress, and doubt are examples of mental blocks shaped by conditioning that keep you from facing a problem. Overcoming your blockages can propel you forward with greater drive and stronger motivation. With such vital energy, you can reach a state of higher performance, better health, and higher goals.

## The All-Encompassing Way

2,600 years ago, Buddha Gautama created a philosophical approach to life that gave hope to humanity through the teachings of transcendence as the solution to human suffering, as well as self-responsibility for one's actions. Buddha's philosophy is still used today, and has spread worldwide, while still remaining in a relatively pure form. Nikola Tesla used his imagination to create devices that we still use in our everyday lives, and instilled one of the most important views on energy management ever discovered. Mahatma Gandhi used peace and non-violence to make significant changes in his society; he provided an example of a highly civilized way of dealing with conflict resolution.

Chinese Emperor Huang Di donated a gift of medical knowledge of immense value for the posterity.

These people are examples of the possibilities of human achievement. They are "super human" in that they have accomplished more than what most humans would, and are "immortal" in that they remain in the actions, hearts and minds of people throughout history. In ancient legends about gods, spirits, idols, totems, or real important people, it is the intention and energy they had that made them honored and revered or simply brilliantly effective and positively influencing.

Indian philosophy describes the phenomenon of the "avatar," or the decent of a collective spirit into one person. In other words, the belief is that some people are seen as carriers of the collective goal and are the personification of a collective mind. By being the quintessence of a group, they not only have the power of the combined synergy of the group, because of the group's love and support, but their intention is fully centered on the advancement of the group as a whole. Just like the cells of a healthy body work in unison for the optimal function of the collective whole, a non-individualistic state of being ensures the mass functions of the organism work cooperatively and cohesively. It is because we have stopped working in harmony that our society has become "diseased.

Creativity, peak performance, maximal functionality, and "super human" conditions can be seen as equal to immortality. Along the same lines, Ernst Becker saw that the state of super achievement, or expanded performance, allows humans to become part of something that will survive the body. The ability to produce something that lasts longer than the physical being is what Becker defines as a "heroic state." Creations, victories,

Remember the 5 External Attitudes of Chapter 6:
   Reject the rejection of your biased conscious mind.
   Expect the tension to arise.
   Accept the tension.
   Detect the patterns of tension and arousal.
   Yield to your subconscious mind to take charge
   and face the problem.

inventions, discoveries, and achievements allow a human being to feel that life has meaning and that he or she is part of a larger scheme or purpose. The more energy put into the objective and the more the aim is to influence a large population, the closer the orientation is toward the top of the Life Goal Scale.

## *Becoming a Hero*

It is important to understand that when you achieve a new clarity of mind, like a young child, you will be highly sensitive to external stimuli and you will easily absorb what is presented to you. We were born with an innate mechanism to imitate our heroes and, as children, we often used this system to copy a figure we perceived to be a reliable model for our survival, like parents and teachers.

When you were a young child, you "downloaded" everything you could from someone in proximity that inspired your awe and admiration. As a child, you didn't have many choices of whom you used as your role model and you did most of your "downloading" subconsciously. Now, as an adult, you can choose what you would like to "download" and from whom. It is therefore important to understand that when you achieve an unbiased conscious mind, you should not repeat the cycle of the past, and you should avoid the negative influences of conditioning.

Instead, choose your influences wisely to "download" what you can from positive role models that coincide with your future orientation and resonance. Once you embrace your resonant way, you can find people, whether historical, current, or fictitious, who have the skills you need to achieve your all-encompassing goals. Discover what these people needed to do to achieve their talents, and then, use your motivation, discipline, and persistence to train yourself into action, while still respecting your innate abilities, talents, and drives.

Harnessing your resonance and direction is not only desirable to achieve your targets, but offers an example for others that reconfirms that great achievements are possible and that there is more to life than mortality. When you think like a hero, you become a hero. When your perception is broad and all-encompassing, you begin thinking for the larger group, to the extent that you can intuitively know what the larger group needs from you and what you can do for them. *The best intention for the larger group is the all-encompassing way.*

"Do not be desirous of having things done quickly. Do not look at small advantages. Desire to have things done quickly prevents their being done thoroughly. Looking at small advantages prevents great affairs from being accomplished."

— Confucius

# Conclusion

*"God gives every bird a worm,*
*but he does not throw it into*
*the nest."*
— *Swedish Proverb*

Returning to the analogy of Chapter 1, you were born an archer continuously facing your future orientation, aiming at your targets. Unfortunately, many obstacles were placed between you and your natural targets and this caused you to misfire. Among the most repercussive obstacles is the virus-like seed of the Persona. This *Evolutionary Glitch*, which is planted in our neural networks by the same mechanisms with which we learn, mature, and develop intelligence, can germinate and grow to become overpowering and controlling. It is up to us to uproot the weeds in our minds: to rise above the root of our problems.

When you carefully read through the pages and do the exercises in this book, use helpful and supportive groups to get you through, and take your time, astonishing results can be achieved. Make sure you really understand the forms of exploitation described in Chapter 2 so you can better avoid them. Get to know your Persona and the Personae of others with Chapter 3. Understand and predict typical reactions of an identified or threatened Persona with Chapter 4. Remove the power the Persona has over you with Chapter 5. Ensure you exercise your inner compass with the help of Chapter 6. Use your feelings and identify your natural resonance with Chapter 7. And expand your goals with an all-encompassing perception while you harness your fear to meet your challenges with the advice of Chapter 8.

With the information and exercises of this book, your technique as an the archer can be greatly enhanced. The process was described in four steps in Chapter 1, each of which can now be accomplished:

Sometimes, the archer reaches a target and then prepares for a new target to emerge, having to, once again, reevaluate his stance, tense the bow, take aim, and let go. It is therefore important to understand that we generally have more than one target to aim for in life and must be mindful of the fact that our stance needs to change accordingly.

Sometimes, the archer gets distracted from the target, aims at something he thinks he should, or makes mistakes in his technique. We should remember that we cannot always be fully separated from social manipulation and that a Persona may want to regerminate with negative social influences. A good archer will acknowledge errors, reevaluate the stance, and find resolution to improve the next attempt to fire an arrow.

Becoming an expert archer requires time, practice, patience, and understanding. It is not achieved overnight. Just like any other skill, diligence, and devotion are needed to learn and improve.

Similarly, an expert archer will not stop performing because a single target has been hit. His passion, enthusiasm, and motivation will encourage him to seek more targets, always keeping up with the challenge.

A first step in the right direction is still only a first step. Don't be afraid of striving ever forward.

---

### The Archer's Technique

1. *The arrow is loaded:* Knowledge is gained.

2. *The bow is held and put into tension:* The Persona is uprooted; new motivations emerge.

3. *The arrow is directed and aimed at a target:* Your future orientation and goal are determined.

4. *The decision of letting go is carefully operated:* You embrace your resonant way, overcome your fears, and propel yourself forward into action.

*"We are what we repeatedly do. Excellence, then, is not an act, but a habit."*

— *Aristotle*

# About the Author

Reflecting on my life, I can remember always having a clear path. As far back as I can recall, I have had an intense passion for Life Force and its phenomena. At a very early age, I can recall my first experiments in chemistry as well as my blooming interest in anatomy and herbology. I remember biology and anatomy books to be my entertainers in childhood.

After a decade and a half in Italy, destiny and a good dose of my stubborn attitude brought me into the metaphysical land of India, the very unfamiliar but mind-challenging country that I immediately took as my principle mentor and educator. There, I remained from the age of 17 to the age of 24, studying for my BAMS (Bachelor of Ayurvedic Medicine and Surgery) before moving to Sri Lanka where I finished my studies in Traditional Chinese Medicine (TCM) and Acupuncture. It was during my additional studies in TCM in Jinan (the capital of the Shangdon province of China) that my clinical work reconfirmed the importance of a Vitalistic approach to medicine.

Modern teaching in India and China combines pathology and physiology with an extensive knowledge of Life Force, which is confirmed and heavily supported by research and studies on millions of cases and experiments. This is, of course, due to the number of patients under study in countries that are extremely populated and to the general approach of research and interest towards these matters.

Oriental medicines, philosophies, and sciences provided me with what I could never find in any other available science in the West: the understanding of Life Force. My scientific thirst for proof was quenched by statistically relevant oriental medical protocols and healing methods. My craving for internal order was completely satisfied by models that could be applied to any phenomena of life. Nevertheless, I always maintained a strong appreciation for Western pragmatism and for the approaches based on efficiency.

Though I was extremely satisfied by my experiences and rewarded with the observation of thousands of patients and a multitude of diseases, I maintained my proof-thirsty attitude and started analyzing the patterns of pathologies from the perspective of Biophysics. I studied Electroacupuncture and Homotoxicology in Germany and realized how a substance, a situation, and a metabolic process can become toxic. I quickly realized that the actions we perform every day play a fundamental role in the state of health or pathology that we encounter and the trend of our symptoms.

After my studies in Germany, my deeper understanding of the importance of electromagnetism and bio-signals brought me to the invention of a microcurrent treatment to promote inner homeostasis through the simulation of the natural "current of injury." It was my purpose to address the deep-rooted issues of patients through effective but non-invasive means.

With years of seeing many cases studies in India and Europe, I also began developing a system that interprets and interacts with complex mechanisms of physiology such as cell reparation and bio-signaling. One of the methods of biological feedback, I dubbed Autonomic Digital Reflex (ADR), gave me a specific insight in the tremendous importance of genetic interaction and interdependence, as well as subconscious processes. I was able to detect several patterns of meaning by accessing involuntary micro impulses from the lumbrical muscles of the hands.

This enlightening experience has brought me further into the understanding that symptoms and events are part of a constellation of signals that indicate our inner condition. Digging deeper into the roots of physical and mental ailments, I found that humans often commit fatal errors that eventually lead to diseases or turmoil. One of these fatal errors is suppressing their symptoms or signs.

Unfortunately, modern medicine has deviated from its wholesome roots and has abundantly dedicated its course to the unwise practice of addressing only the symptoms and not the root cause of diseases. Humans, as well as doctrines, also keep these errors in place and defend them strenuously by their way of being, even when faced with the discovery of their faulty and dangerous nature. It doesn't take much to see this commonly revealed to you by any smoker or alcoholic who regularly justifies their bad habit.

During the ten years I spent in New Zealand, I began to

research physical and mental behavior as the outcome of an internal state and started building artificial intelligence computer programs in order to analyze how an intelligent system learns, what it learns, and how it uses what it learns. The result of these years of research was startling: I came to understand that the roots of our problems derive from the way our biological system learns. This element was crucial to my knowledge of human behavior and was so astounding to me that I reoriented my entire research into a mixed path of medicine, philosophy, and information sciences.

My life, and the life of the many people around me, changed dramatically bio-chemically, socially, emotionally, and physically. I discovered that human subconscious processes operate and react in resonance and in relation to a physiological way that is hindered by an "evolutionary glitch" of our cortex, the same error against which our forefathers had been warned. This is our Ego, our Persona, our internal error. This error has many faces that can be seen, mapped, analyzed, and counteracted.

The processes to heal or mend from this root of problems had profound effects on my state of being that changed me physically and mentally. I wrote this book with the hope that other people could undergo the same transforming experience.

# References and Resources

1. James, O. (2007). *Affluenza*. Vermilion.

2. Zimbardo, P. (2007). *The Lucifer Effect: Understanding How Good People Turn Evil*. Random House.

3. Pavlov, I. P. (1927). *Conditioned Reflexes: An Investigation of the Physiological Activity of the Cerebral Cortex*. Oxford University Press.

4. Domjan, M. (2003). *The Principles of Learning and Behavior, Fifth Edition*, Thomson/Wadsworth.

5. Giacomo R., et al. (1996). Premotor cortex and the recognition of motor actions. *Cognitive Brain Research, 3*, 131-141.

6. Bandura, A. (1977). *Social Learning Theory*. Prentice Hall.

7. Dawkins, R. (1976). *The Selfish Gene*. Oxford University Press.

8. Veblen, T. (1899). *Theory of the Leisure Class*. Macmillan.

9. Lowenstein, K. (1973). *The Governance of Rome*. Nijhoff.

10. Gouldner, A.W. (1973). *The Politics of the Mind*. Basic Books.

11. Frankl, V. (1984). *Man's Search For Meaning*. Washington Square Press.

12. Frankl, V. (1984). *Man's Search For Meaning*. Washington Square Press, p.104.

13. Gennep, A. (1960). *The Rites of Passage*. Routledge & Kegan Paul.

14. Bergson, H. (2003). *Creative Evolution*. Kessinger.

15. Lakhovsky, G. (1991). *The Secret of Life: Cosmic Rays & Radiations of Living Beings & Electro-Magnetic Waves*. Gordon Press.

16. Hameroff, S. & Penrose, R. (1998). *Toward a Science of Consciousness: The First Tucson Discussions and Debates*. MIT Press.

17. Pribram, K. (1991). *Brain and Perception: Holonomy and Structure in Figural Processing*. Lawrence Erlbaum Associates.

18. Becker, E. (1973). *The Denial of Death*. Simon & Schuster.

19. Solomon, S., Greenberg, J., & Pyszczynski, (2004). The cul-

tural animal: Twenty years of terror management, theory, and research. In S. Solomon, S.L. Koole, and T. Pyszczynski (Eds.) *Handbook of Experimental Existential Psychology*. Guildford Press.

20. Frankl, V. (1984). *Man's Search For Meaning*. Washington Square Press, p.166.

**In addition to the references within the text of this book, the following are some interesting reads that have greatly contributed to my current understanding of life and its functions:**

◆ Bergson, H. (1911). *Creative Evolution*. Henry Holt and Company.

◆ Becker, R. (1982). *Electromagnetic Fields and Interactions*. Blaisdell.

◆ Becker, R.O., & Selden, G. (1985). *The Body Electric: Electromagnetism and The Foundation of Life*. Quill/William Morrow.

◆ Bentov, I. (1988). *Stalking the Wild Pendulum: On the Mechanics of Consciousness*. Inner Traditions International.

◆ Bertalanffy, L. (1973). *General System Theory: Foundations, Development, Applications*. G. Braziller.

◆ Bohm, D. (1980). *Wholeness and the Implicate Order*. Routledge & Kegan Paul.

◆ Burr, H.S. (1972). *Blueprint for Immortality: The Electric Patterns of Life*. Neville Spearman.

◆ Capra, F. (2004). *The Hidden Connections: A Science for Sustainable Living*. Anchor Books.

◆ Capra, F. (1996). *The Web of Life: A New Scientific Understanding of Living Systems*. Anchor Books.

◆ Capra, F. (1982). *The Turning Point: Science, Society, and the Rising Culture*. Simon and Schuster.

◆ Chenglie, L., Liangwen, G., Tianchen, L., & Jiasen, Z. (1989). *A Collection of Confucius' Sayings*. Qi Lu Press

◆ Gerber, R. (1996). *Vibrational Medicine: New Choices for Healing Ourselves*. Bear & Company.

◆ Grof, S. (1993). *The Holotropic Mind: The Three Levels of Hu-*

man *Consciousness and How They Shape Our Lives.* HaperCollins Publishers.

- Hardy, C. (1998). *Networks of Meaning: A Bridge Between Mind and Matter.* Praeger/Greenwood Publishing Group.

- Jahn, R.G. & Dunne, B. (1987). *Margins of Reality: The Role of Consciousness in the Physical World.* Harcourt Brace Jovanovich.

- Krebs, C. & Brown, J. (1998) *A Revolutionary Way of Thinking: From a Near Fatal Accident to a New Science of Healing.* Hill of Content.

- Laszlo, E. (1996). *The Systems View of the World: A Holistic Vision for Our Time.* Hampton Press.

- LeDoux, J. (2002). *Synaptic Self: How Our Brains Become Who We Are.* Viking.

- Lipton, B. H. (2008). *The Biology of Belief: Unleashing the Power of Consciousness, Matter & Miracles.* Hay House.

- Marshall, I. & Zohar, D. (1990). *The Quantum Self: Human Nature and Consciousness Defined by the New Physics.* Morrow.

- McTaggart, L. (2002). *The Field: The Quest for the Secret of the Universe.* HarperCollins Publishers.

- Oschman, J.L. (2000). *Energy Medicine: The Scientific Basis.* Churchill Livingstone.

- Penrose, R. (1995). *Shadows of the Mind.* Vintage Press.

- Penrose, R. (1990). *The Emperor's New Mind: Concerning Computers, Minds and the Laws of Physics.* Oxford Press.

- Popp, F-A, Becker, G., Konig, H.L., & Peschka, W. (1989). *Electromagnetic Bio-Information.* Urban & Schwarzenberg.

- Sheldrake, R. (1995). *The Hypothesis of a New Science of Life: Morphic Resonance.* Park Street Press.

- Sheldrake, R. (1988). *The Presence of the Past.* Fontana/Collins.

- Talbot, M. (1996). *The Holographic Universe.* HarperCollins.

- Voll, R., & Schuldt, H. (1977). *Topographical Positions of the Measurement Points in Electro-Acupuncture.* ML-Verlag Uelzen.

# Index

Affluenza, 18

Albedo, 118, 126-130
Conjunction, 127, 128
Fermentation, 127, 128-129
Distillation, 127, 129-130
*see also Alchemy*

Alchemy, 117-119
*see also Albedo, Nigredo, and Rubedo*

Anomie, 36-40, 120

Attitude, 3, 4, 9-14, 17, 22, 30, 37, 117, 131, 132, 138-140, 154-155, 159, 168, 178-179
Internal, 140-142
External, 142-154, 162, 188

Belonging, 1, 11-12, 35, 142-145, 150, 159, 168, 173, 179

Bilious Persona, 39, 82-87, 106, 122
Animal Analogy, 86
Coping Strategy, 106
Effects on the Body, 86
Gender Differences, 85-86
Goals, 86
Interaction with Others, 84-85
Probable Reaction, 87
Temperament, 82-84

Brain, 21, 25, 36-47, 108, 138, 140, 142, 161, 184
*see also R-Complex*

Brainwash, 18

Buddha, 181, 187

Buddhism, 2, 42, 117
Four Noble Truths, 49

Cell / Cellular, 29, 42, 47, 130-131, 138, 161, 168, 186, 200

Challenge, *see Self-Challenge*

Cognitron, 121, 124

Confucius, 12, 117, 139-140, 181, 191

Conscious, 24, 27-29, 39-43, 48, 101-102, 108-110, 117, 119, 123, 130, 131, 137, 148-150, 151, 161, 168, 185, 189
Collective Conscious, 27, 39
In History, 41-42

Preconscious, 184
Subconscious, 29, 41, 48, 101-102, 123, 131, 137-138, 142, 148-150, 153, 161, 167, 174-176, 185, 187-188
Superconscious, 146
Conspicuous Consumption, 24-26
Conditioning,
Classical, 19-20
Operant, 20
Separate from, 30
Social, 4, 18, 28-31, 35, 40, 97, 101, 162, 173, 175-176
Coping Strategies, 102-112
Apprehension, 104
Confusion, 103
Depression, 105
Frustration, 106
Immobilization, 106
Resentment, 104
Resolution, -107-112
Cytoplasma, 160-161
Death,
Denial of, 173-174
Reminders, 175
Dendrite, 108-109
Education, 18, 29-30, 165
Ego Structure, 41
Élan Vital, 159, 174
Engram, 109
Evolution, 3, 40-42, 102, 138, 159
Eustress, *see Stress*
Fear, 38, 41, 101, 142-145, 151-153, 173-176, 184-187
In the Media, 23
Of Death, 173, 175-176
Of Failure,
of Rejection, 142-145, 151
Of Responsibility, 184
Of Shame, 184
Of Uncertainty, 153
Overcoming, 184-187
fMRI, 25
Gestalt, 163

Goal, 17, 35, 46, 139, 152, 160-162, 174, 180-181, 182, 195, 196
    Assessing, 167-168
    Determining, 166-167
    Life Goal Scale, 181-184, 189
    Of Each Persona, *see individual Personae*
    Problems, 9-13, 26, 147
Habituation, 27, 35
Hero,
    Becoming a, 189
    Heroic State, 188
    System, 174-176, 182, 184
Identification, 158-162
Lao Tzu, 184
Leisure Class, 24
Life Continuation, 176
Life Goal Scale, *see Goal*
Lucifer Effect, 18, 40
Lymphatic, 58-63, 104, 122
    Animal Analogy, 63
    Coping Strategy, 104
    Effects on the Body, 62-63
    Gender Differences, 61
    Goals, 61-62
    Interaction with Others, 60-61
    Probable Reaction, 63
    Temperament, 58-60
Mask, *see Persona*
Media, 17, 25-27, 28-, 29, 31, 175-176
Melancholic, 39, 74-80, 105, 122
    Animal Analogy, 79
    Coping Strategy, 105
    Effects on the Body, 78-79
    Gender Differences, 78
    Goals, 78
    Interaction with Others, 76-77
    Probable Reaction, 79-80
    Temperament, 74-76
Memetics (memes), 23-24, 29-30, 44
Mind, *see Conscious*
Mirror Neurons, 21

Microtubules, 161

Motivation, 10-12, 125, 131, 139, 142, 159, 162, 173-176, 179, 180, 181, 187, 196

Nervous, 39, 66-71, 104-105, 122
    Animal Analogy, 71
    Coping Strategy, 104-105
    Effects on the Body, 70-71
    Gender Differences, 69
    Goals, 69-70
    Interaction with Others, 67-69
    Probable Reaction, 71
    Temperament, 66-67

Neural Network, 42, 43, 108-112, 122, 124, 127, 144, 161, 195

Neuron, 21, 108-109, 161

Neuromarketing, 25-26

Nigredo, 118, 119-126
    Calcination, 120-121
    Dissolution, 120, 121-123
    Separation, 120, 123-126
    *see also Alchemy*

Oniomania, 25

Oxytocin, 38-40

Patterns, 17, 43, 109, 128, 148, 162, 188
    Behavior, 122-123
    Thought, 43, 120, 123
    of the Persona, 101-102, 108
    *see also Wave Patterns*

Persona, 36-48, 122-123, 166-167
    Sanguine, *see Sanguine*
    Lymphatic, *see Lymphatic*
    Nervous, *see Nervous*
    Melancholic, *see Melancholic*
    Bilious, *see Bilious*
    Phlegmatic, *see Phlegmatic*

Phenotype, 9, 138

Phlegmatic, 39, 90-95, 106-107, 122
    Animal Analogy, 94-95
    Coping Strategy, 106-107
    Effects on the Body, 94
    Gender Differences, 93-94

Goals, 94
    Interaction with Others, 91-93
    Probable Reaction, 95
    Temperament, 90-91
R-complex (reptilian brain), 184-187
Rejection, 35, 36-40, 43-44, 45, 49, 120-121, 184
    Rejecting Rejection, 142-145, 188
Resonance, 159-163, 167, 179, 180, 189, 195
Resonant Wave Patterns, *see Wave Patterns*
Rubedo, 118, 130-132
    Coagulation, 131-132
    *see also Alchemy*
Rules of Thought, 2, 42, 48, 56, 93, 101-102, 108, 120, 123, 132
Sanguine, 39, 52-56, 103, 122
    Animal Analogy, 55
    Coping Strategy, 103
    Effects on the Body, 55
    Gender Differences, 54
    Goals, 54-55
    Interaction with Others, 53-54
    Probable Reaction, 55-56
    Temperament, 52-53
Seed (of Persona), 36-44, 120-121
Self-Challenge, 3-5, 97, 117, 155, 167, 175, 181, 184-186, 196
Sensitization, 27, 35
Signs, 43, 102, 110, 128-129, 131-132, 142, 153, 162, 163, 166-
    167, 179, 185
    Accepting, 148-150, 162
    Expecting, 146-148
    Patterns, 151-152
Skepticism, 153-154
Stance, 3, 9-13, 48, 108, 139, 145, 150, 155, 159, 162, 179, 196
Stockholm Syndrome, 24
Stress, 1, 35, 38, 39, 80, 104, 105, 185-187
    Eustress, 185
Talent, 1, 137
Thermal Noise, 161
Wave Patterns, 163-166
    Expanding, 165
    Impacting, 164

Intensifying, 166
Rising, 165
Soothing, 164
Standing, 1165
Synchronizing, 164
Yielding 165-166
*see also Patterns*
Virtue, 139
Virus,3, 23-24, 28-30, 42, 44, 46, 97, 120, 195
Mental Virus, *see Memetics*
*see also Seed of Persona*

*For more information on
seminars and presentations
by Albert Garoli and his team,
and to learn more about other
books, services, and products,
please visit
www.TheEvolutionaryGlitch.com
and
www.holonomics.info*